MATERIAL WORLD

Perri Lewis

MATERIAL WORLD

The Modern Craft Bible

www.eburypublishing.co.uk

2 4 6 8 10 9 7 5 3 1

First published in the United Kingdom in 2012 by Virgin Books, an imprint of Ebury Publishing
A Random House Group Company

www.randomhouse.co.uk

Addresses for companies within The Random House Group Limited can be found at
www.randomhouse.co.uk/offices.htm

The Random House Group Limited Reg. No. 954009

A CIP catalogue record for this book is available from the British Library

MIX
Paper from
responsible sources
FSC™ C004592

The Random House Group Limited supports The Forest Stewardship Council (FSC®), the leading international
forest certification organisation. Our books carrying the FSC label are printed on FSC® certified paper. FSC is
the only forest certification scheme endorsed by the leading environmental organisations, including Greenpeace.
Our paper procurement policy can be found at www.randomhouse.co.uk/environment

Designed by www.ninaziegler.co.uk

Printed and bound by Firmengruppe APPL, aprinta druck, Wemding, Germany

ISBN: 9780753540657

To buy books by your favourite authors and register for offers, visit www.randomhouse.co.uk

CONTENTS

'DON'T FRET TOO MUCH ABOUT THE RULES'

'I am a material girl'

MADONNA, 1985

I'm one of those people who make stuff. I always have been; ever since I can remember I've painted, drawn, sewn, knitted and made. In the past, I've always been the odd one out, the only girl with the handmade T-shirt. And necklace. And bag. And hat.

Not any more, however. The friends of mine who, even a couple of years ago, claimed not to be the making type, have since changed their tune. Like me, every now and again they walk straight past Topshop and into the John Lewis haberdashery department to lust after paper and fabric, not dresses and shoes.

Craft might have had a big moment in the early 2000s, when Rachael Matthews and her Cast Off craft group were getting thrown out of The Savoy for knitting too loudly, and every other celebrity was claiming to knit or sew, or both, but its real time is now. Young women knitting in pubs or making their own dresses don't make the news any more; no longer considered unusual, it has become something else people just do.

CONTINUED OVERLEAF

LONG LIVE THE MATERIAL WORLD

Trends rise and fall ever quicker these days, so it's interesting that after ten years in the spotlight, craft is still huge. Why? Enforced austerity seems the most likely candidate and, certainly, the recession had something to do with it. Scaremongering headlines about the economy would have driven many a cash-strapped lady to mend rather than replace, renovate instead of throw out.

But the rise of craft began before the financial world crashed and, despite popular assumption, making things yourself isn't actually that thrifty. Sure, it's cheaper to mend something than to buy a replacement, but try sewing a (good-quality) dress for the same price as a high-street equivalent – you won't be able to. So what's going on?

Our conscience definitely has a hand in craft's new-found popularity. Make something from scratch and you needn't worry about whether or not it was handmade by children in the developing world who are being paid a pittance (page 14 has all you need to know about keeping your materials green). And just as we're tiring of cheap Primark tat, so, too, are we fed up of looking exactly like the rest of the country. Buy from the high street and you risk having the same outfits and home as everyone else. Learn how to wield a needle and thread, however, and what was an identikit armchair/coat/handbag can become something that no one else in the world owns. Crafts are also more accessible than ever. Craft shows are back on the telly, high-street giants are selling materials again, craft groups and shops can be found in most towns and cities, and we're seeing the rise of a new breed of craft venue: the workshop-cum-studio-cum-rent-a-sewing-machine café (see my favourites on page 222).

All this is feeding the already-thriving social side to craft. Sewing circles might have been around forever, but today's craft scene is massive. As our local communities disappear, it seems we're reaching out for replacements to fulfil our need for connections, human contact and a sense of belonging. (Learn everything you need to know about craft groups on page 100). The web has had a massive part to play in all this too, giving lone crafters stitching away in their bedrooms access to huge, friendly groups of like-minded people across the world. (Find my crafters' guide to the net on page 64–6.) On the flip side, as we spend more and more time in a virtual world we spend less engaging with actual things. But the actual act of making cannot be done online: picking up a pair of scissors or a piece of paper forces you to connect to the offline, non-virtual world of the here and now, which can have a wonderfully positive impact on your well-being (this new hobby of yours has health benefits too, see page 39).

Step away from the ladies making their own dresses and cushions and there's another side of craft that's stealthily growing, too. On the web, on the streets and in the galleries many a maker is taking traditional craft techniques and twisting, subverting and playing with them so that they become almost unrecognisable to us. These crafters exploit the fact that many of us still associate stitching with our grannies and use this preconception to marvellous effect.
You'll meet plenty of these people in this book: guerrilla knitters (page 87), artists (page 138 and 176) and even activists – or 'craftivists', as they're more appropriately called (page 125). The more weird and wonderful things these guys do with craft, the more people are inspired to pick up the skills and take them one step further.

There could be another thousand reasons as to why craft continues to reign supreme, but for me, there's just one that's kept me coming back to the sewing box: it gives me a brilliant excuse to flex my creativity.

I might have a bookshelf full of craft books, packed with step-by-step instructions for how to make everything from toilet-roll lampshades to couture rip-off dresses, but I rarely follow the projects word for word. I'll use the first few lines instead, to remind myself how to master a basic technique, or stick to the last paragraphs, so I get the finish as neat as it is in the picture. The rest I'll work out by myself, drawing on my own knowledge of what works and what doesn't, and what might just be a more effective/cheaper/better way of doing it. I always end up making something that is absolutely right for me, rather than going through the motions, following instructions for something from a book that's almost, but not quite, what I wanted.

I like to think of this as the Jamie Oliver approach to craft. Whack in a bit extra of what you fancy and cut back on the elements you don't like or don't have handy. Don't fret too much about the rules along the way; the important thing is that what you end up with is perfect for you.

It's why this book is not like most craft books. I've not filled it with step-by-step projects that you must follow word for word (like craft-by-numbers). Instead I'll teach you 15 different techniques so you can go away and use these to make whatever you what, however you like it.

The structure of each chapter is simple: I show you the basics (because without those even Jamie couldn't experiment well), then I'll hand over to experts who will explain how to make something average look sensational (and not remotely *Blue Peter*-esque). We're very fortunate that some of the world's leading designers, makers and artists in fashion, interiors and craft have agreed to share their ideas, advice and inspiration with us. These guys are at the top of their game, so it's well worth taking note of what they say. Then there's a project (you didn't think I'd leave you entirely to your own devices, did you?) and plenty more suggestions for things to make now that you're well versed in that particular technique. (Did you know that once you had learned how to print a T-shirt you could create personalised wallpaper, too?)

Beginners, this book is designed to get you running with scissors. You might like to follow each step-by-step project carefully until you're confident enough to experiment on your own (and remember, you might not get it straight away, but you will, with time). As you grow as a crafter, I hope this book grows with you and becomes less of an instruction manual and more of a book of inspiration. For those of you who are old hands at this craft malarkey, I'd like to think this book will help you to take your making to the next level. Perhaps you want to discover new ways to use existing skills, or master a technique you've once tried but not quite got the hang of? Either way, I hope *Material World* finds a place on your bookshelf.

Perri

The basics

Everything you need to get your craft on

The materials

There's no need to waste loads of cash on craft tools straight away: invest in a basic kit, then add a few luxuries to it as and when you need to.

THE ESSENTIALS

SEWING NEEDLES
Buy a multi-pack that contains assorted sizes.

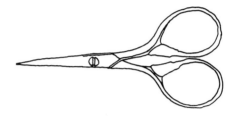

SEWING
SCISSORS

THREAD
Look for all-purpose, cotton sewing thread. A beginner's kit should include one reel each of black and white and also a couple of your favourite colours. Don't fork out for a rainbow set from the off, but buy different-coloured threads as and when a project requires them.

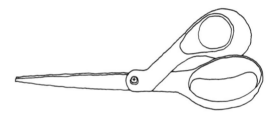

FABRIC SCISSORS

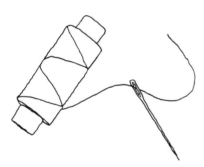

SCISSORS
Ideally you'll have three pairs: sewing scissors (often called needlework or embroidery scissors) with a short, sharp blade; a pair of fabric scissors with a long, sharp blade; and an all-purpose pair for cutting paper and card. Use a pair for the wrong task and you'll find they cut badly and get blunt faster. You have been warned.

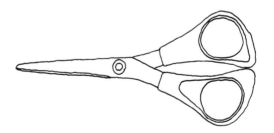

ALL-PURPOSE
SCISSORS

PINS

Long, sharp ones with ball-shaped coloured heads are the most versatile.

TAPE MEASURE

Because rulers can't measure around curved things.

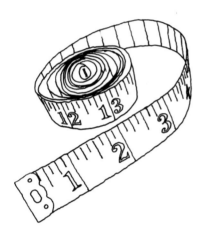

TAILOR'S CHALK/
WATER-SOLUBLE MARKERS

Either is fine for marking fabric. It is better to use these than a pencil or pen, which will leave pesky, difficult-to-remove marker lines all over your newly-made stuff.

IRON

To press fabric and seams.

PENCIL AND RUBBER

Choose a soft lead pencil, as its marks rub out more easily than anything harder.

RULER

Go for a basic, 30cm (12in) long, see-through one.

GLUE

A glue stick, an all-purpose white glue and a tube of superglue should cover it.

GLUE STICK

ALL-PURPOSE WHITE GLUE

SUPERGLUE

TAPE

A roll of sticking tape and a roll of masking tape always come in handy.

PAINTBRUSHES

Set aside a couple of cheap ones, especially a fine one, for using with glue.

THE LUXURIES

NEEDLE THREADER
Worth every penny if you never thread a needle first time.

THIMBLE
Protects your thumb when sewing (although I find them difficult to use).

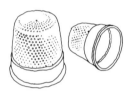

PINCUSHION
You can keep your pins in the box they came in, or you could treat yourself to a pretty pincushion. It keeps them all in one place and the ends free from dirt.

STITCH PICKER
Misplaced stitches *can* be removed with a pair of sewing scissors, but a stitch picker is easier to use and less likely to tear the fabric.

SEWING MACHINE
Buy one for £50 or £5,000, how much you pay depends on what you want it to do with it. For basic tasks like sewing seams, cheaper ones will do the job, but consider how much you'll use it, and whether you'll want more from it in the future. It's often worth investing £100–£200 in a good-quality machine with a range of functions rather than £50 on one that you'll grow out of in a few months. Singer, Janome, Bernina and Elna are good brands.

SEWING-MACHINE SUPPLIES
Check what accessories your machine comes with, but you might want to buy a few spare bobbins (to wrap different-coloured thread around, particularly for the most-used colours), a lint brush (to clean dust from the machine's motor), extra feet (different tasks require different feet) and different-sized needles (for sewing different types of fabric).

BOBBINS

PINKING SHEARS
Use these zigzag-edged scissors to cut fabric so it doesn't fray.

METRE RULE
For when your projects are bigger than 30cm.

DOUBLE-SIDED TAPE
Less messy than using glue to stick paper to paper.

GLUE GUN
Because hot glue doesn't have a best-before date (and is infinitely more fun to craft with).

CRAFT KNIFE, METAL RULER AND SELF-HEALING CUTTING MAT
Craft knives cut paper with more precision than scissors, so they are especially good for fiddly paper cuts or when you want to cut a very straight line.

IT'S NOT EASY BEING GREEN

Crafting something from scratch is infinitely better for the environment than buying it ready-made, but imagine how much greener it would be if your materials were eco-friendly, too …

✂ *'Follow the four-step eco rule'*, says **Kelly Rand**, founder of *craftingagreenerworld.com*. 'Do you really need it? Can you buy it second-hand? Can you make it yourself? Is there a recycled option?' If you can't say yes to any of these, consider altering your craft project so that you can, she advises.

✂ *Check the fine print.* 'Look for organic certification where possible – chemical inputs will be minimal on these products,' advises **Ellie Langley**, a felt artist who runs craft classes at Slackhouse Farm, the greenest B&B in the UK (*fleecewithaltitude.co.uk*). 'Papers should be FSC or PEFC certified.' The Fairtrade mark covers some craft products, too, including yarn, fabric and paper.

✂ *Invest in the right tools.* 'Not only do you get scissors, knitting needles and embroidery hoops for a steal if you buy them second-hand, but many of these items will look amazing in their vintage shape,' says Kelly. But, if you do have to buy new, choose scissors, needles and pins with recycled metal content.

✂ *'Think carefully about new fabric,'* suggests textile artist **Ruth Singer**, author of *Sew Eco: Sewing Sustainable and Re-Used Materials* (*ruthsinger.com*). 'It is hard to be definitive about the best sustainable material. Organic cotton is grown and processed without the potentially harmful chemicals used in conventional production, and uses less energy and water,' she explains. But synthetic fabrics take even less water and energy to produce and take fewer resources to keep clean, so some consider them sustainable. (They are not, however, made from sustainable materials or are biodegradable.) Then there are sustainable fabrics such as bamboo, soya and Tencel. These are made from renewable plant sources and have intentionally low-impact production processes, but the raw materials may not be organic or Fairtrade. 'It's a bit of a minefield,' Ruth explains, 'but think about which element is most important to you when you buy.'

✂ *'Go local,'* advises Ellie, whether it's for scissors made in Sheffield or paper made from Welsh sheep poo. 'We still have real craftsmen in Britain and the quality of their products is infinitely higher than the mass-produced, cheap, imported rubbish.'

BUILDING YOUR STASH

Deciding what fabric, thread, gems or ribbon to fill your craft box with is one of the most delightful jobs you'll have to do. But although materials are now more readily available than ever, they don't always come cheap. Many a crafter has taken a few precious morsels of crafting paraphernalia to the till, only to be stung by an unexpectedly hefty bill when it's all added up.

So I take a slightly different approach to stocking my craft box, which leaves me with a decent wedge of cash to splash out on a few good-quality things I really want (usually classic Liberty-print fabric, VV Rouleux ribbons and handmade paper from Paperchase).

✁ *Hit the high-street sales.* It's not unusual for high-end beads and buttons to be sold for a pound a piece in specialist craft shops, so snap up reduced necklaces and bracelets for a couple of quid in the high-street sales (Accessorize is the best for this). Cut them up and you'll have much more than your money's worth in craft materials. The same goes for belt buckles, handbag straps or clothes made of fabric you like (I've been known to buy a top for a fiver just to rip the fake diamond embellishments off the front).

✁ *Use the charity shops.* Many of these stock fabric, yarn, thread and paper donated by crafters who are clearing out their stash. Or buy cheap jewellery or clothes to cut up (this is a great place to find leather).

✁ *Look carefully at your packaging.* Stuff from fancy shops tends to be packaged beautifully. Cut off ribbons, gems, embellishments – even save the cardboard if it's pretty. Store similar-looking stuff in plastic tubs in your craft box or clear plastic folders in a ring binder, so you can find it easily.

✁ *Save your birthday stuff.* People spend a fortune wrapping presents in gorgeous paper, so resist the urge to tear it off quickly and instead open presents carefully and keep the packaging for future projects (I'm not being a killjoy, I promise). Don't throw away birthday cards unless you've cut off any interesting designs or embellishments first.

✁ *Take the free samples.* Whether it's fabric off-cuts in a furniture shop, or paint-colour cards in the DIY store, keep an eye out for freebies that you can take and use. It's about being a magpie and thinking imaginatively about what you might be able to work with in the future.

THE ART OF SWAPPING

Another smart way to increase your craft stash is through swapping – a practice which has grown in popularity over the last few years. Perhaps you've inherited a box of white velvet but really need some blue silk ribbon, which you know a friend has but will never use. Learn the rules of the swap and everyone leaves happy.

Keen swappers **Barley Massey** of Hackney craft emporium Fabrications (*fabrications1.co.uk*), and **Amy Twigger Holroyd**, founder of the Keep and Share knitwear label (*keepandshare.co.uk*), share their wisdom …

✂ *'Get creative with your assets,'* Amy says. 'As well as things you've made, you might swap lessons [perhaps your crochet skills for their screen-printing knowledge] or creative services such as web design, or even other random stuff. A woman once told me that she'd done a swap with her grandma – giving her a primer in microbiology in exchange for a beginner's knitting lesson.'

✂ *'Trust is vital,'* explains Barley. 'Start with friends or trusted members of your community,' she recommends. 'If you decide you want to enter into an exchange with a stranger, you may want to check out their capabilities. But in essence – trust your instincts.'

✂ *'Be smart when you ask,'* advises Amy. 'If you fancy doing a swap, ask in such a way that the other person won't feel awkward saying no. And don't be offended if they do say no, particularly if they are running a business – unfortunately, lovely swaps don't pay the rent. Equally, if you're approached and don't fancy it, don't feel obliged,' she says. 'If you're not up for it, you could say that the other person's work is fab, but doesn't suit your personal style. Or – if you sell your work – that you need to concentrate on cash sales.'

✂ *'Everyone is equal,'* Barley believes. 'Everyone's skills are considered equal, irrespective of market value. Swaps are gauged by the amount of time taken to finish something, or the loan of tools or facilities. On bigger projects it is fair to log hours and monitor as you go. And if materials need to be purchased, then this needs to be agreed and paid for somehow.' The key, Barley and Amy agree, is that you're both happy and get a fair deal. No one should feel hard done by.

✂ *'Agree a time frame,'* says Barley. 'Otherwise neither of you is clear when you have to complete the swap. You could even get together at different times and see how the swap is progressing: this is a nice way of building a new friendship.' Make the most of the fact this is a more meaningful exchange than just parting with your cash.

The essential techniques

So, you've got all the kit – now it's time to use it.
There are a few essential techniques that are good
to have under your belt, most of which are for
needleworking crafts.

HOW TO ... THREAD A NEEDLE

Sure, it's the most basic of sewing tasks, but it's
also one that can stump the beginner and be oh-so
frustrating for even well-versed crafters. Wet your
thumb and forefinger with your tongue and use these
to flatten the end of the thread; now it's easier to
poke through the eye of the needle (this is especially
important when you're using fat embroidery thread).
Or, get yourself a needle threader: poke the wire
diamond all the way through the needle's eye, poke the
end of the thread through the diamond, then pull the
diamond out. Voila! The thread is threaded.

START AND FINISH A LINE OF HAND SEWING

Tie a little knot in one end of your thread and, for
extra security (particularly when sewing seams and
buttons), sew a few stitches over each other before
you embark on a line; this stops the thread from
unravelling should the knot somehow come undone.
What to do when you've finished a line? Take your
thread to the back of the fabric and sew three or four
very small stitches over the top of the last stitch you
made. For a little extra security, knot the thread before
you snip off the extra.

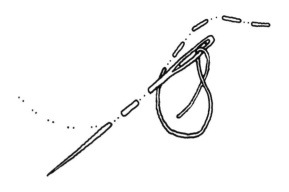

SEW A RUNNING STITCH

Pass the needle in and out of the fabric, keeping the
stitches on top the same length. The stitches at the
back should be equal in length, too, but half the size
of those on top.

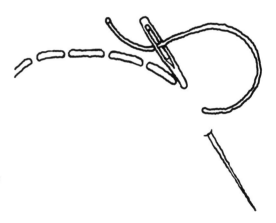

SEW A BACKSTITCH

The most useful stitch in your sewing arsenal: it's
super-strong, so brilliant for seams. Sew one stitch and
poke the needle up through the fabric as if you were
about to do a line of running stitch, then take
the needle back to meet the end of the previous stitch,
and so on. Learn this one and you'll go far.

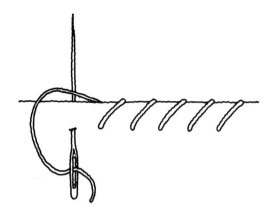

SEW AN OVERSEW STITCH

This one's for sewing two edges together. Poke the needle through both pieces of fabric, a couple of millimetres from the edge. Take the thread over the top and back through both pieces of fabric again. Keep the stitches neat, even and on a slant.

TACKING

This is a temporary line of stitches designed to hold two pieces of fabric together before you sew them properly. Essentially, it's a long running stitch in a contrasting thread colour so that it can be seen and unpicked easily. (I must confess, I prefer tacking to using pins.) This technique is also known as basting.

START AND FINISH A LINE OF SEWING-MACHINE STITCHES

You've got two methods to choose from: use the first when the stitching won't be seen (i.e. when sewing seams) and the second when the stitching will be visible (machine embroidery, for example).

Sew your first few stitches then put the machine into reverse and go back over them. Repeat this once more, then continue stitching as usual. When you get to the end of the line, the same rule applies: put it in reverse for a few stitches, come back, then reverse and come back again. Snip off the excess thread.

The second method is more tricky to execute, but looks far nicer. Start off as above, but don't put the machine in reverse, and then continue stitching until you get to the end. Don't reverse here, either; just stop and cut the threads with at least 5cm to spare. Thread the top thread on to a hand sewing needle and poke it through the fabric to bring the thread to the back. Tie the top and bottom thread together using a couple of knots, and trim. Do the same at the beginning of the line.

SEW AROUND A CORNER ON A SEWING MACHINE

Stitch along the straight edge until you reach the corner: stop the machine, making sure the needle is still inserted in the fabric – this means your stitches will stop and start at the same point. Raise the foot. Now you can easily rotate your fabric until it's facing the way you need it to. Lower the foot and you're ready to stitch the next part of your project.

USE AN EMBROIDERY HOOP

This is a natty little invention. You get two hoops: one larger (and adjustable), one smaller (and not). Lay your fabric over the smaller hoop then whack the larger one on top, tightening it to get the fabric taut. Fabric pulled tight like this is much more comfortable to embroider. (Don't put felt in an embroidery hoop – you'll stretch it – or textured fabrics, such as velvet, as it will leave marks).

USE FABRIC STABILISERS

These look a bit like sheets of paper and are used to, yes, stabilise or support fabric. This is necessary when you're doing lots of stitching on it, or it's stretchy and would otherwise be difficult to control. Tack the stabiliser to the underside, or buy 'topper' stabiliser, which you tack to the front of the fabric (this keeps stitches from sinking into dense material).

How to remove a stabiliser? There are four different types: ones you cut away, tear away, wash away or heat away (with an iron). The first two leave remnants of stabiliser there, the other two get rid of it completely. Which type you use depends on the project. Follow the instructions on the packet, of course, but these two rules will serve you well: 1. The thicker the fabric, the thicker the stabiliser that is needed. 2. If a project is delicate and can't be ironed or washed, you'd be silly to use wash-away or heat-away stabilisers.

SEW ON A BUTTON

It won't have escaped your attention that there are two types of buttons available: those with holes in the centre and those with loops at the back (the official term for this is a 'shank').

First, the two-holed or four-holed button. If the button is going to be fastened through a buttonhole (as opposed to being there just because it looks nice), lay a matchstick or thick needle on top of the button before you sew.

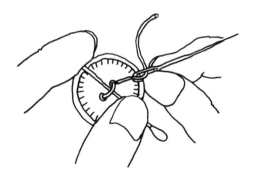

This means the button won't sit flush to the top of the fabric, so there's room for a second piece of material to fit around it without straining the thread that's attaching it.

To sew, hold the button in place with your finger, poke the needle up through one hole, and down through another (taking it over the matchstick if you're using one). Repeat this three or four times (alternate equally between the holes on a four-hole button), then secure the thread at the back of the fabric.

If you've used a matchstick, remove it *before* you secure the thread; the button will be a little loose, but that's how it's meant to be. Wrap your thread around the line of thread that sits between the button and the fabric, as below, then take the needle to the back of the fabric, and secure.

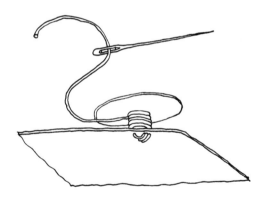

To sew on a shank button, push your needle up through the fabric, take it through the loop, and then push it back down through the fabric again. Repeat a few times, then secure the thread.

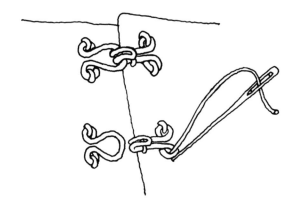

SEW ON A PRESS STUD

These things come in two pieces that interlock to create a super-strong fastening. The ones with holes in can be sewn on: simply hold in place with your finger and stitch through them a few times. The ones that don't have holes need a special press to set them; this can be bought from most craft shops.

SEW ON A HOOK AND EYE

This is the kind of fastening you get at the top of a zip on a high-street skirt (which promptly falls off two minutes after you've bought it). The two pieces should be positioned exactly opposite each other, on the underside of the fabric (where they won't be visible), and sewn on so that only the hook and the eye stick over the edge. Stitch over each loop a few times, then secure the body with a few stitches, too, so that it doesn't flap around.

ADD FUSIBLE WEBBING

An invention we should all be grateful for – especially if you don't actually like sewing very much. Instructions vary a little between brands, but essentially this sits between two pieces of fabric and the heat of an iron bonds them together. (Some come with a paper backing, which are useful for appliqué, see page 211.) The trick is not to use steam or move the iron back and forth, but to place it down and lift it up. Make sure the edges and corners are bonded properly – they're the last bits to stick.

SEW SEAMS

When stitching two pieces of fabric together, you must sew 1cm ($^1/_2$in) from the edge. (Were you to sew just one or two millimetres away from the edge there's every chance the fabric would fray and the stitches would no longer hold the two pieces together.) It's why whenever you cut out a piece of fabric that will be sewn to another you must always add 1cm ($^1/_2$in) extra all the way around. Say you want a purse that measures 40cm by 60cm (16in x 24in) – you'd better cut a piece that is 42cm by 62cm (17in x 25in).

Alas, this extra fabric sometimes gets in the way. Turn a freshly sewn bag, purse, dress, etc., around the right way and the extra fabric is too bulky for the corners to look sharp and for the curves to sit nicely. This is when you need to snip the seam allowance.

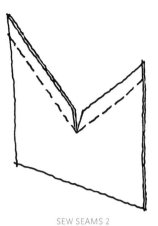

SEW SEAMS 2

✂ *On corners.* Slice a triangle off the end, at least 3mm from the stitching (see below). Or for inside corners, cut a thin V (see right, top).

✂ *On curves.* Snip V-shapes into the seam at even intervals (again 3mm). The width of the V depends on whether you have an inside or outside curve from the stitching (see right, middle and bottom).

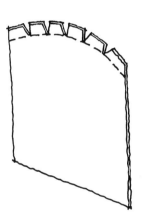

SEW SEAMS 3

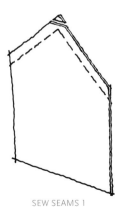

SEW SEAMS 1

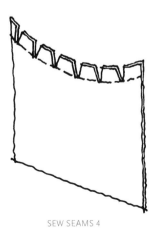

SEW SEAMS 4

TRANSFER A PATTERN

We're not all a dab hand with a pencil, but in craft, that's OK. If you love a pattern or image you find in a magazine or online, use one of the following techniques to transfer it on to fabric, ceramics or wood. Then you can just stitch or paint inside the lines.

✂ Invest in a sheet of carbon paper and lay it carbon-side down on your material. Lay your design, right-side up, on top of the carbon paper and draw over the lines of your pattern with a pen or sharp pencil. Press hard so that the carbon leaves the paper and sticks to your material. Be sure not to move either sheet of paper while tracing, or lean on it too hard – otherwise it'll rub the carbon on to the material. As carbon paper comes in dark and light colours, choose a shade that contrasts with the material you're working with.

✂ The cheaper method is to use tracing paper. But, I must warn you that it's fiddly and – unless the design is symmetrical – you'll need to flip it first. To do this, trace the pattern, then turn the tracing paper over and lay it on a clean piece of white paper. Draw over the pencil lines you made, pressing hard, so the image is transferred to the paper in reverse. Now trace this flipped image. Finally, lay this new piece of tracing paper on to the fabric/ceramics/wood, pencil-side down, and draw over the lines, transferring the pencil marks to the material the right way around. Phew! See? I told you this wasn't easy.

Remember, just because a design you love isn't the perfect size, you can still use it. Scan it and alter the size on a computer, or use a photocopier to shrink or enlarge it.

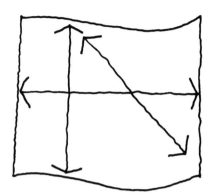

WORKING WITH FABRIC

✂ *How to cut it:* You'd think that you just chop it up and then you're ready to go. Not so. Look closely at your material. See? It's made up of woven strands that go horizontally and vertically (unless, of course, you've got non-woven fabric, such as felt, and then this rule doesn't apply). Cut along these lines and the piece of fabric you get won't be any different to the piece of fabric you cut it from. However, cut it diagonally – along the 'bias' – and your cut piece will be stretchy. Throughout the book I'll tell you when you need to cut something 'on the bias'. When measuring fabric to cut, use the neat, finished edge (known as the 'selvedge') to measure from, else you risk getting an odd-shaped square or rectangle. When you buy fabric off the roll, you can't guarantee that it has been cut in a straight line, but the selvedge always will be.

✂ *How to iron it:* Pressed fabric is about a million times easier to work with, but when you're using stuff that doesn't take well to a hot iron, be careful, or else you'll be left with gunk all over the hotplate. Iron felt, wool and synthetics on a very cool temperature and, for the most delicate stuff – silk, chiffon, etc. – lay a piece of clean, thin, iron-able fabric over the top (a tea towel usually does the job) and iron over that.

'BEG, STEAL OR BORROW!'

Unlock your creativity

Does the thought of a blank canvas leave you tingling with excitement or full of dread? For many people – even the most experienced crafters – making something without a set of instructions to follow is just too daunting a prospect to consider. Too many of us assume that if you're not a 'creative type' you couldn't possibly come up with anything better than what's already out there.

But I don't believe in this 'creative type' business. The only difference between so-called creatives and the rest of us is that they know not to panic and where to start. And, wonderfully, that is something any of us can master with the right techniques up our sleeve. So to help you learn the fine art of starting from scratch, I asked two of my favourite designers to tell me how they fire up their imaginations …

In 2010 **Donna Wilson** was named Designer of the Year at the British Design Awards, and her cushions, ceramics and creatures are now sold across the world (*donnawilson.com*).

✂ *Start a sketchbook – and carry it with you.* 'If an idea pops into my head, it means I can jot it down wherever I am.' Donna likes to flick through old ideas too: 'I see if there's anything more in them. Sometimes you are in more of a creative mood so you've got loads of little ideas, but you don't actually develop them into anything. So it's nice to go back.'

✂ *Be snap happy.* 'Instead of always looking at second-hand imagery from books or blogs or magazines, it's really important to use your own eyes and take photographs of things you like,' Donna believes. 'If you're out shopping and a combination of colours catches your eye, take a snap of it on your phone for reference.'

✂ *Pressure is not your friend.* 'When I'm under pressure I can't design,' she admits. 'Then it gets stressful, because I think, "I've got to get these designs done". To do my best work I've got to clear my head and get a bit of peace and quiet.' She has some sound advice: 'Don't put yourself under too much pressure to come out with something really good straight away. I'll have loads of ideas that are crap, and then one or two will start to work. Eventually it will just click, so keep going.'

✄ *It's OK to mix it up.* 'Sometimes I will cut up bits of paper and do a collage; other times I might do a watercolour or some knitting or a sketch. For me, a lot of the creative process is about generating imagery. So don't feel you have to play with thread when designing a piece of embroidery, or paper when designing a paper craft: crack out whatever materials you feel comfortable with and start with them.'

'THERE'S NO HARM IN COPYING AT FIRST'

Everyone knows an **Emma Bridgewater** coffee mug or plate when they see it; the Oxford-based designer has created one of the most iconic ranges of ceramics of the last decade (*emmabridgewater.co.uk*).

✄ *It's not a mountain, it's a molehill.* 'If you think of designing as a blank page, it's bloody daunting,' says Emma, 'so remind yourself that it's not a blank canvas. Because you have a lot to bring to it: skills – you might be neat with your hands or have a feeling for colour – and you'll already have loads of ideas in your head.'

✄ *Beg, steal or borrow.* 'There's no harm in starting by copying,' she says, 'especially if you're not confident in your own ideas. If you're doing something in textiles, go to a textile museum, go to sales at Bonhams. One thing that helps is telling yourself that there's nothing new – "I'm not copying, I'm recycling".'

✄ *Get by with a little help from your friends.* Emma designs with her husband, Matthew. 'The best things we do are collaborative. We will sit and talk about what's working, what we like. It's really important to do this.' Ask friends/family/strangers at a craft club what they think of your ideas, and it should spark a fair few more.

✄ *Stick to your strengths.* 'How you design will depend on what your strengths are. Some people are spectacularly hopeless at colour, so it would be foolish for them to be trying to do colour-block designing,' she says. Instead, Emma suggests you should focus on the outline of a design, the shapes you're using, and stick to black-and-white or two-colour, depending on what you feel comfortable with. 'For my mother-in-law, Pat Albeck, designing is very much built on her colour sense, whereas with Matthew it's all about line drawings.'

✄ *Be a lifelong collector.* 'Rather than sitting down at an empty table, line up inspiring items in front of you so that you've got company. That might be a series of Polaroids, scraps from magazines, things you've photocopied out of books, or whatever. Building up a visual reference is absolutely vital. I collect stuff and I buy junk endlessly – textiles, books, ceramics.' Print images from blogs that inspire you, keep any packaging that you love and buy trinkets that inspire ideas.

'BE
PATIENT'

Embroidery

*So you think stitching is all about naff teddy-
bear patterns and old-lady pastels? Think again.
Get it right and embroidery can look contemporary
and stylish (and, once you get the hang of it,
it's really not so hard).*

The technique

MATERIALS

1 Fabric

Essentially, anything goes, but cotton is easiest, linen is good and felt is sturdy. Try silk, satin and stretchy fabrics when you're more experienced. Don't restrict yourself to plain materials, because you can – and should – embroider on patterned fabric too.

2 Embroidery hoop

(SEE PAGE 14)

3 Sewing scissors

(SEE PAGE 11)

4 Dressmaker's chalk

(SEE PAGE 12)

5 Stitch ripper

Not essential, but easier than scissors for unpicking mistakes.

6 Stabiliser

(SEE PAGE 18).

FOR HAND SEWING

1 Embroidery needle

This is sharp with a decent-sized eye, because embroidery thread is thicker than sewing thread.

2 Embroidery thread

This is made up of six strands of thread twisted together; you can buy thread made from cotton, wool, silk and other materials. Use two strands for finer details, or six if you want thick stitches. To split the thread neatly for finer embroidery, pinch one end between your fingers, then pull off the required number of strands.

FOR MACHINE SEWING

1 A sewing machine

As long as you can drop the feed dogs, any machine will do.

2 A darning foot /free-motion embroidery foot

A special machine foot for embroidery.

3 Needle

A topstitching needle is best, as it's finer and sharper than universal needles.

4 Thread

Use anything you can find that's suitable for machines.

GETTING STARTED

Your first port of call is page 18; use this information to work out whether you need to use fabric stabiliser or not. Then give whatever you're embroidering a good iron (sorry, there's no avoiding that) and put it in your embroidery hoop. For machine embroidery, the hoop is used slightly differently: the fabric goes right-side *down* over the small hoop, and so is essentially used upside down.

EMBROIDERING BY HAND

Whatever you're embroidering, start with the outline, build up the middle section, and leave the finer details until last. Here are a few of my favourite stitches, but look on the internet or in any good embroidery book and you'll see there are hundreds more to play with.

OUTLINE STITCHES

Running stitch: see page 17

Backstitch: see page 17

Stem stitch: Gives the illusion of rope. Lightly draw a line on your fabric and insert your needle to the left of it from the back. Make a diagonal stitch, pushing the needle back through the fabric to the right of the line. Repeat all the way up, keeping the stitches the same length, with no gap in between them. Change the angle of the stitch if you want the line to be thinner or thicker.

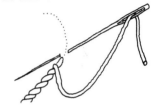

Chain stitch: Poke the needle into the fabric from the back and pull it through to the front. Make a loop with the thread and use your thumb to hold it in place. Poke the needle back down through the fabric, next to where the needle just came through. Bring it up again just inside the loop, and when you pull the thread firmly this loop will be held in place. Repeat above the stitch to make the second loop and so create the look of a chain.

FILLING STITCHES

Seed stitch: Sew equal-length stitches randomly, at different angles, inside an outline. The closer together they are, the more dense the filling will look.

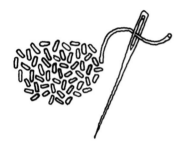

Satin stitch: Lightly draw the shape you want to fill. Start in the middle (it's easier to begin with the biggest stitch) and insert the needle just outside the edge of the line. Sew a stitch across the shape, pushing the needle down just outside the line. Repeat until the shape is filled, keeping the edge of the shape even and the strands of thread untwisted.

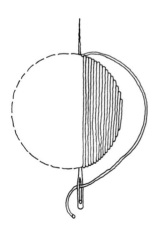

DECORATIVE STITCHES

French knot: It's not easy to master, but it is worth learning. Take the needle through the fabric from the back to the front, then wrap the needle around the thread three times close to the fabric.

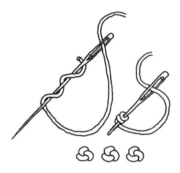

Push the needle back through the fabric, right next to where it first came out, and keep hold of the thread with your other hand, keeping it taut. Pull the needle down slowly, and as the thread disappears to the back of the fabric, it'll form a little bobble on the front. (While the thread is moving, use your finger to hold the three loops close to the fabric to create the perfect knot.)

Daisy stitch: Take the needle up through the back of the fabric, then down again a few millimetres, keeping a loop of thread at the front (your thumb can hold it in place).

Secure that loop with a little stitch at the top. To create a flower, repeat this stitch a few times in a circle.

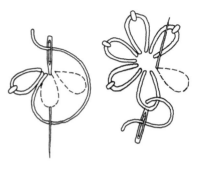

COMMON PROBLEMS

My embroidery thread always gets knotted. You're cutting it too long. And, after every few stitches you should let the needle dangle and the thread untwist. Use the sharp end of a needle to unpick knots, if they're too tight, snip the thread under the knot, bring the thread to the back of the work, and secure.

DOING IT WITH A MACHINE

Set your machine up the right way and even the cheapest model can do fancy free-hand embroidery. Swap your usual foot for a darning foot, switch to medium tension and lower the feed dogs (your manual will show you how). Dropping these means that you're in charge of moving the fabric, not the machine. Set it to straight stitch.

Start with some scrap fabric (in the embroidery hoop, of course) and play around making shapes and patterns; machine embroidery takes some getting used to, so practice is essential. Hold the hoop steady with both hands, one on either side, but make sure you are relaxed and sitting comfortably. Try sitting close to the machine, or putting your elbows on the table – whatever works best for you.

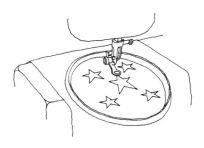

Put your foot down and sew quickly, so the stitches are close and even, but move your hands slowly. Fluid movements, not short, jerky ones, are best. Try to complete designs or patterns without stopping, using one length of thread, but it's not the end of the world if you don't. When you're happy with the design, stop the machine then tie off the thread (as described on page 17).

A straight stitch is perfect for outlines, but experiment with the other stitches your machine can do. To fill in shapes, either work methodically, as with satin stitch, and fill in using rows of stitches with little or no gap in between (straight stitches with thicker thread work well, as do rows of more decorative stitches – zigzag, for instance.) Or freestyle it and scribble stitches inside the lines. Either way, there's no need to cover every last bit of fabric with stitches; even a few lines gives the impression of a shape being filled in.

COMMON PROBLEMS

I can see the bobbin thread on the top of my work. Change the bobbin thread so it's the same colour as the top-stitch thread. Or decrease the tension of your top stitch.

My thread always gets tangled at the back. It sounds like it's time to clean the needle and bobbin area of your machine, to get rid of the dust and lint. If that doesn't work, refer to your manual.

FINISHING OFF

Lay the embroidery face down, cover with a tea towel, then iron.

STITCH A PHOTOGRAPH

So you want to make a stitched version of a picture you love? Simple. You can transfer a design on to fabric in three easy ways.

- ✂ *Trace it.* Hold up the design to a window, lay the fabric on top, and draw over the outline with tailor's chalk or a soft pencil. This is the cheapest way to trace a design, but it's no use if the fabric is thick or a dark colour.

- ✂ *Use carbon paper* or tracing paper: see page 22 for how.

- ✂ *Use dissolvable paper* or dissolvable stabiliser. Lay this on top of your pattern, trace it, then lay it on top of your fabric. Secure with tape or pins and embroider over it. When you've finished, put the fabric in water and – as if by magic – the paper or stabiliser will disappear. Obviously this is the pricier option, but it's brilliant for detailed machine designs done on washable fabrics (page 18 has more details on fabric stabilisers).

The masterclass

ELISABETH ROULLEAU

ON COUTURE EMBROIDERY

COMMISSIONED BY DIOR, CHANEL AND HERMÈS
TO CREATE EMBROIDERIES, ELISABETH ALSO
TEACHES HAUTE-COUTURE EMBROIDERY AT
CENTRAL SAINT MARTINS. *elisabethroulleau.com*

MOVE AWAY FROM TRADITION

Although you can do great things with plain embroidery thread, it's not the only material you can use. 'If you embroider with a wool thread, a stitch is going to look completely different,' she says. 'My students love working with ribbon, too.' (In haute-couture embroidery you use a hook, not a needle, but both materials could be used with a large-eyed, sharp needle threaded with a needle threader.) Elisabeth suggests working the same stitch in different materials for a contemporary-looking design.

GET EXPERIMENTAL

'I ask students to bring in different materials – threads, fabrics, coins, little stones, even pieces of wood that are not too heavy – and create something with them. It is an exercise in creativity.' She believes that knowing how to attach peculiar objects to fabric beautifully, without glue, means you will be better able to work decorative objects like *paillettes* (small foil discs) and precious stones into your designs.

LOOK TO THE MASTERS

'Keep your eyes open for embroidery,' she advises. 'When you are looking in magazines, notice the techniques that are being used.' Fashion and interiors magazines don't tend to show close-ups of embroidery, but on their websites you can often zoom in to inspect the stitching.

BE PATIENT

Embroidery is not something you can rush. 'Don't be impatient. In this world, where everything is fast, embroidery is a world apart. If you need 12 hours to embroider something, it's not possible to do it in three.' Scale down your project instead of trying to rush it if time is in short supply.

INSIDER TRICKS

'If you use a sewing machine for long periods of time, secure your machine at an angle. I have mine tipped towards me, so I can see what I'm stitching without being hunched. There is a bolt under my machine, which I attached to a handmade wooden ramp.'

GILLIAN BATES, TEXTILE ARTIST

gillian-bates.com

TUGBA KOP

ON MIXING EMBROIDERY WITH PAINT
THIS ILLUSTRATOR DOESN'T STITCH EVERY LAST DETAIL
OF HER WORK, BUT USES PAINT AS WELL AS THREAD
TO CREATE PRETTY, WITTY ACCESSORIES AND PRINTS.
tugbakop.com

CHOOSE ACRYLIC

'I prefer using acrylic paint to fabric paint; it's more versatile, easier to control and comes in a larger range of colours. You can turn regular acrylic into fabric paint by mixing in something called "textile medium". Use it as it is for a solid colour, or water it down for more of a light wash.' Do check the instructions on the paint packet to make sure it can withstand water, if you are using it on a garment or something that may need to go in a washing machine regularly.

ADDING THE COLOUR

'When you add the paint depends on the desired effect. Should you want it to look more spontaneous, paint the fabric in roughly the right place and then stitch over it – I like this misaligned. Or, if you want the colour to be within the lines, then carefully paint inside your already-stitched shapes.'

THIS IS NOT A DRAWING

'You don't have to stick to black thread and coloured paint. Personally I never use black because I find it too harsh. Try clashing the colours of the paint and the thread for a more striking image.'

'Often, more interesting stitching comes from using two single strands of different shades of the same colour threaded through the eye of one needle. Or, use two completely different colours of thread.'

EMMA COWLAM, EMBROIDERY ILLUSTRATOR
emmacowlam.com

'My embroidered portraits of people are so heavily stitched that I always work on a heavy cotton, so it can take the weight.'

JENNIFER ANDREWS, EMBROIDERY ARTIST
childrenplayingwithfire.wordpress.com

'Transfer vintage colouring books, tattoo designs or children's drawings to fabric and embroider over them: the lines are simple, and so easy to stitch.'

JENNY HART, FOUNDER OF SUBLIME STITCHING
sublimestitching.com

The project

PIMP YOUR KEY RING

You don't have to have slaved away at a piece of embroidery for it to be great; this tiny project is quick, satisfying and useful.

HOW HARD IS IT TO DO?
As hard as you make it.

HOW LONG DOES IT TAKE?
An evening, unless you're replicating the Mona Lisa in miniature.

MATERIALS

1 **Pen**

2 **Paper**

3 **Felt**

4 **Thread**

5 **Needle**

6 **Ribbon**

7 **Key ring hoop**

STEP 1
What do you fancy on your key ring? You can have anything. As you know from page 22, even if you can't draw it, you can easily transfer a picture you love on to fabric and stitch it. Once you've got your idea, draw it on to a larger piece of felt (say, 20cm x 20cm/8in x 8in) with tailor's chalk/washable pen, or transfer it using one of the methods explained on page 22. Just make sure it's no bigger than 8cm (3in) (really, anything bigger on a key ring just gets in the way).

STEP 2
I know on page 18 I say not to put felt in an embroidery hoop, but in this case it's OK (although the rest of the piece will be stretched and possibly ruined, the 50p or so that it'll cost you is worth it because embroidery hoops make stitching things so much easier). Follow the outlines with running stitch, fill in the sections with French knots, do the whole thing on a machine – do whatever you like! If you mess up, or decide you don't like it halfway through, no sweat – it's such a small project that you can just start again. (There is just one thing to remember: if your keys take a bashing in the bottom of your bag, avoid satin stitch or other large stitches; keep them small and they'll be less likely to get snagged.)

STEP 3
Once you're done, cut around the design, leaving 5mm (¼in) extra. Cut a second piece of felt too, exactly the same size as this embroidered piece.

STEP 4
Cut a short piece of ribbon and fold it in half. Lay it on top of the second piece so that the loop sticks out the top. Stitch it in place, neatly, using backstitch.

STEP 5
With the embroidered piece right-side up, lay it on top of the second piece, so the ribbon is sandwiched between them. Using a matching piece of all-purpose thread, oversew the two pieces together (or, use one of the leather work stitches on page 143 – this will ensure the key ring looks nice and tidy from both the back and the front). Slip a key ring on to the ribbon loop and your keys are ready to be pimped.

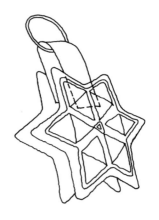

The extras

EMBROIDER A NECKLACE

Hang your embroidered masterpiece on a wall and, sure, it'll brighten up your room. But, hang it around your neck and it'll turn a plain outfit into something very special indeed.

You've got instructions for making a fabric necklace on page 182, so work from that; try to create an embroidered version of a couture necklace you love (gems created with satin stitch look beautiful), or take inspiration from beautiful patterned fabric.

Embroidered earrings look ace, too: stitch them on to an earring-sized piece of felt and oversew a second piece on the back to hide the messy stitches. Then, punch an eyelet through the top and slip a jump ring through it (see page 180). An embroidered pendant is made the same way. Don't have an eyelet tool? Stitch your felt straight on to a jump ring.

SCRAP THE FABRIC

Paper is a brilliant alternative to material. Machine sewing on paper is easy peasy, so long as you use the tying method (page 18) to secure the thread (or, ditch the thread altogether and use your machine to create a pretty little line of holes – it works best when teamed with collage on the front of a birthday card).

Hand sewing works too, but you'd be wise to punch the holes first to make the sewing part as painless as possible (lay your paper on an unwanted book and poke the paper with a needle to make the holes where you want them). If you're making a card, stick a square of card over the back of the embroidery to cover the messy ends. Making a batch of cards/invites/posters? Photocopy, scan or photograph your embroidery and print off as many as you need.

Alternatively, you can embroidery anything that has holes in it; wicker baskets or vases with decorative holes, for example. And if something doesn't have holes, drill them! I've seen people embroider wooden doors/chairs/desks/bowls/necklaces – even a car bonnet. If you can drill a line of holes in a surface, you can stitch it. Just remember you might need something thicker than embroidery thread, though. Fancy a trip to the DIY store for thin rope, anyone?

THE MODERN MONOGRAM

Don't we all love things that have our name on? You could go down the classic route of decorative initials (print out some fancy letters, use the transferring method on page 22, and sew them using satin stitch and metallic thread). Or do something a little more contemporary: I like joined-up handwriting done with a simple backstitch (if you've got a steady hand, you can write straight on to fabric with tailor's chalk). If you simply must embroider initials on to dressing gowns or towels (in an ironic manner, I'm assuming), remember to wash the garments first and tack heavy tear-away or cut-away stabiliser on the back and wash-away stabiliser on the front before you start to sew. (This will prevent the stitches sinking into the toweling.) See page 18 for more stabiliser advice.

CREATE SOME FUNCTIONAL ART

Anything made from fabric can be given a makeover with a few stitches: cushions, bedspreads, napkins, bags, babies' bibs, clutch bags, PJ holders, T-shirts, dining-chair pads ... the list goes on. Think creatively about where you can show off your new stitching skills, but remember to think before you stitch. Although some people can create incredible embroidery freestyle, my work always turns out best when I've sketched it out on paper first. Either work with the existing pattern of the fabric (stitch around the outline of shapes, for example) or ignore it completely. Remember, designs don't have to be sewn on to plain white cotton to look brilliant.

'MOVE AWAY FROM TRADITION'

Craft your way to happiness

Pundits always put the rise in interest in craft down to the poor state of our finances. Piffle, I say. Making really isn't that thrifty unless you're using toilet rolls and sticky-back plastic (and that's never a good idea if you're older than five). Craft is, however, a fantastic way to boost your mood and combat stress …

The antidote to fraught day at work is always a little crafting (I only crack out a cheeky glass of wine on a Friday, honestly). With every stitch, fold or snip I make, the thoughts buzzing around my head start to slow down. My attention soon turns from the stresses of the day to the problem at hand. How do I get this awkward button to stay in place? Can I really sew 147 red sequins on that dress before Saturday night?

Certainly, I'm not the only one who reaches for their materials the moment the worry sets in; I'm yet to meet a devout crafter who doesn't rave about the therapeutic virtues of their hobby. But how does it actually work? That's where **Betsan Corkhill** comes in. Having noticed an onslaught of anecdotal evidence about the feel-good effect of craft, the physiotherapist-turned-knitting-therapist set up Stitch Links in 2005 (*stitchlinks.com*), an organisation dedicated to researching what's actually going on when we make.

'It's the rhythmic, repetitive movements that are important,' Betsan says. While mindlessly stitching away you can be transported to a meditative state. 'People describe it as escaping into a peaceful sanctuary where their mind is set free from problems.' **Dr Joanne Turney** of Bath Spa University, who studies the psychological impact of textiles, agrees. 'Like a metronome, the rhythm of working the same stitch over and over again mediates our heart rate and our breathing,' she says, 'creating a feeling of stability, calm and inner quiet.' But of course, not all crafting is as peaceful or rhythmic as

sewing a line of backstitch. (Try balancing a laptop on your knee while following a complicated pattern online, all while stitching a hat in a tiny flat.) No worries, says Betsan, for this can be meditative in its own way, too. 'It's a type of meditation that depends on concentration – like a mantra.' Get immersed in creating a birthday card and your brain gets distracted from some of your stress and worries – some even believe it helps to block out physical pain, too.

THE STRESS FACTOR

So even the making that leaves you flinging scissors across the room in frustration does wonders for your brain. 'Mastering new skills brings novelty into your life,' says Betsan. 'And novelty helps to build new brain skills.' The better you become at finding solutions to craft problems, the more your problem-solving skills are honed; Betsan believes that this helps you become more psychologically flexible. The most psychologically flexible among us are those who are able to cope with anything life throws at them. Methinks a battle with a tricky seam or stitch is a small price to pay for such a reward.

Alas, this doesn't all land in your lap the moment you pick up a needle and thread. 'Be prepared to learn, practise and persevere to reap these benefits,' advises Joanne. 'Think of it like yoga: at your first lesson it's a nightmare; you fall over and wonder how it can be relaxing. But you're not born with that ability to be calm and still and in tune with your body. It takes effort and time.'

But once you've cracked it, boy is it good. Delicious feelings of satisfaction creep up the moment that last red sequin is stitched on (even if you might have just done battle with 146 of them). 'It's your brain's reward system kicking in,' explains Betsan. 'Put effort into a task and it's successful, and the reward system fires off and gives you a boost of feel-good chemicals.' It's a wholly unfamiliar feeling for so many us. Because in modern life, when do we ever get to actually finish anything? Clear your inbox and a minute later it's full of emails again. Craft is different. 'It is measurable. That is very important. There is a very obvious end to our efforts,' says Joanne.

THE BEST MEDICINE

The simple act of craft can counteract more of modern life's negatives, too. As uncertainly grows – in the security of our jobs and the level of our overdrafts – our lives seem more out of our control than ever before. But learn to create something yourself, and you wrest back a little control. 'Having command of your world, in whatever form that takes, can be extremely therapeutic,' Joanna believes.

That craft involves using our hands offers a unique set of rewards as well, as in today's society most jobs require us to do precious little physical work. Betsan explains: 'Hands have got a huge representation in the brain, so activities that involve them creating a tangible product stimulate our reward system far more.' Introduce a little making into your life and you give your brain more opportunities to make those feel-good chemicals.

And as we become more accustomed to living in the digital world, chatting to friends on Facebook rather than over a cup of coffee, craft can help us re-engage with the real, physical part of our lives, too, something that many a psychologist has recommended for enhanced well-being. 'It brings us back to the here and now,' she says. 'It gives you a sense of engagement in a way that many of us have lost with the everyday world.' You can liken it to the ancient but newly popular concept of mindfulness, where being acutely aware of the way things smell, taste, touch and feel is being taught

to everyone from the depressed teenager to the burnout CEO to counteract stress and anxiety.

What craft really does, then, is help us foster connections – to the real world, and to others, too. Making is universally and historically a social activity, and as Betsan says, it 'creates cohesion with others and a sense of belonging'. The girl who has just moved to a new city where she doesn't know anyone can shake off feelings of isolation if she joins a craft group, or even just strike up a conversation about knitting with a fellow crafter on Twitter.

I reckon there's enough there to persuade anyone to pick up a needle, pen or a pair of scissors. You might think it a little odd that I've not yet mentioned the feel-good effect of actually creating something you love yet, but that's because what you craft is pretty much irrelevant. It's the making that makes making so good for you.

Découpage

The humble piece of paper has more potential than you ever knew: use it for revamping everything in your home, from furniture to jewellery, telephones to shoes, by using this age-old technique.

The technique

MATERIALS

1 Paper

Specialist découpage papers are available, but I think great designs are hard to come by, so try maps, newspapers, comics, stamps, pages from books and other thin papers. Print your own designs, but only using a laser printer (ink-jet runs when you cover it with glue).

2 Découpage glue

Buy it in gloss, matte or antique finishes, or use a 50/50 mix of PVA glue and water, which will dry clear.

3 Scissors/craft knife

Small, sharp scissors are fine for most projects, but if you have a super-detailed image, use a craft knife and mat.

(SEE PAGE 130 FOR HOW TO USE IT PROPERLY)

4 Brushes

Use wide brushes for applying glue to large pieces of paper and fine brushes for small, detailed pieces.

5 Varnish

Choose a waterproof, clear, polyurethane varnish suitable for wallpapered surfaces. Not always essential for smaller projects.

6 Lint-free cloth

Because it doesn't leave fibres behind, you are less likely to get bits stuck between layers of découpage.

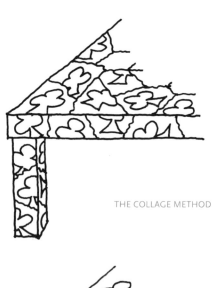

THE COLLAGE METHOD

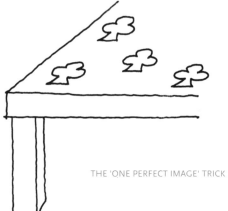

THE 'ONE PERFECT IMAGE' TRICK

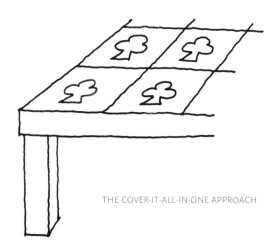

THE COVER-IT-ALL-IN-ONE APPROACH

GETTING STARTED

Give the surface you'll be sticking the paper on to a good clean with a lint-free cloth, or warm water and washing up liquid if it's particularly dirty.

THE COLLAGE METHOD

Rip up or cut up loads of bits of paper: how big each one is depends on what you're covering. Start with one piece, somewhere near the centre of your object. Cover the back with découpage glue and stick down, smoothing out any wrinkles. Add a second piece in the same way, either slightly overlapping the first (if you like the carefree look) or aligned with it (if you like order, neat lines, or are generally a bit anal about these things). Continue until the piece is covered.

THE 'ONE PERFECT IMAGE' TRICK

Think carefully about your image. Is it possible to cut it out? (Some are just too fiddly.) Colours are important, too: a dark image on a black surface won't show up, while anything bright and bold will look great on a white background. Now to consider positioning: would it look best in the centre, or to the side? Play around until you're happy, then take a photo to refer to.

Apply a thin layer of découpage glue to the back of the picture. Stick the centre of it down first (tweezers can help if it's very intricate), then work your way to the outer edges, using the palm or side of your hand to smooth it down. Wipe away any glue that oozes out before it dries.

THE COVER-IT-ALL-IN-ONE APPROACH

Using this technique, one flat side of an object is covered with a single sheet of paper. Is this strictly découpage, or just a version of wallpapering? Perhaps it's the latter, but I'm not sure it matters.

Measure the size of the surface you're covering using a set square and ruler (there's nothing shabbier than an ill-measured piece of paper stuck on). Use these measurements to make a template from newspaper first; check it fits, then cut out your proper piece of paper. Apply a thin, even layer of glue to the back. Line up one edge of the paper with one edge of the object, and carefully stick it down, working away from this edge. Use your hand to stick down the rest of sheet, making sure it's aligned with all the edges of the surface you're covering and that any crumples are smoothed out instantly. Mop up any excess glue that squeezes out of the sides straightaway.

FINISHING OFF

Once the glue has set, add a coat of découpage glue to the entire surface of the object (not just over the single image), and leave to dry. When it is completely dry, give the surface a wipe, add another layer of glue, and allow it to dry again. Repeat this a few more times. A final layer or varnish might be appropriate, too, for tabletops or anything else that suffers a lot of wear and tear.

COMMON PROBLEMS

I've got a bubble. Push the air out with a damp sponge if the glue hasn't dried. If it has, make two slits in a cross-shape in the centre of the bubble, peel back the four sections carefully and re-glue flat.

I've stuck the wrong piece of paper in the wrong place. Rather than peeling it off – and risking ripping the paper – let it dry, then cover it with a new piece. (It's always wise to have more paper to hand than you think you'll need.)

The masterclass

LOU ROTA

ON WORKING WITH CERAMICS
LOU IS THE QUEEN OF MODERN DÉCOUPAGE. LIBERTY
SNAPPED UP HER FIRST LINE OF DÉCOUPAGED FURNITURE AND
ANTHROPOLOGIE LOVED HER ICONIC DÉCOUPAGED PLATES SO
MUCH THEY ASKED HER TO DESIGN A RANGE FOR THEM.
lourota.com

DON'T USE STANDARD PAPER

'I use Lazartran waterslide decal paper,' she says. This is because ink printed on this becomes water resistant. Lou sends her designs off to be printed professionally, but you can buy Lazartran for home printers. Remember that any image you print needs to be reversed, so when it's added it appears the right way round. 'Be original: take your own photographs and play around with them in Photoshop.'

CHOOSE CERAMICS WISELY

'If the glaze on your plate has cracked, when you put it in the oven the yuck will come out of those cracks and bubble up under your decals.' Always go for more pristine-looking china when using it for découpage.

IT'S ALL IN THE PREPARATION

'I flash my Lazartran paper very quickly in a hot oven for no more than 15-30 seconds,' she advises. Once cool, cut out the pieces and put them in a bowl of tepid water. While they're soaking, clean and dry your ceramic thoroughly.

THINK ABOUT THE DESIGN

'How you position images on ceramics is hugely important. You're creating a scene, not just slapping something on,' Lou reminds us. 'Work with the colours, design and shape that are already there. If I want the image to go around a curve of a plate, I heat the curve with a hairdryer first, so it's easier to stretch the image over it.' Lay the images in position, printed side down, and remove any air bubbles with your fingers or a small squeegee.

FIRE IT UP!

'Let the decorated ceramic dry out in a domestic oven set on a very low temperature for about 20 minutes,' she says. 'Every 15 minutes, turn up the temperature until you get to about 200 degrees. Then you let it cool.' What you're left with is a ceramic with a hard, shiny surface that can be very carefully hand washed (but never with a scour). Think of it as something decorative for the wall or to place a few cakes on, rather than to eat your spaghetti bolognese off.

THE ALTERNATIVE

You can, of course, just découpage ceramics with paper, glue and varnish. 'They're possibly more durable; you just have to accept they're not to be used for food.'

INSIDER TRICKS

AMELIA COWARD

ON DÉCOUPAGING WITH FABRIC

BEFORE WOWING THE WORLD OF INTERIORS WITH HER INCREDIBLE PAPER DÉCOUPAGE ART AND HOMEWARES, WHICH HAVE FEATURED IN ALL THE MAJOR HOMES MAGAZINES, AMELIA USED TO CREATE AND SELL FABRIC-COVERED FURNITURE. *bombus.co.uk*

CHOOSE THE RIGHT MATERIALS

'Use a tightly woven cloth to stop the adhesive saturating through; plain woven cotton is perfect. Thin fabrics are OK, as long as they are very tightly woven (actually, thick upholstery fabrics are more troublesome on curves and corners), but avoid silk, satin weaves or anything with a sheer or shiny surface,' Amelia advises. 'Instead of découpage glue, we use a gum- or rubber-based adhesive, such as Copydex.'

CUT IT DIFFERENTLY

Fabric is more complex to work with than paper. Sections need to be cut as if they are being tailored to the object you are covering, rather than just using randomly sized pieces. Amelia adds, 'You will typically work with larger pieces of fabric than you would with paper.'

COVER IT DIFFERENTLY

Be careful when folding fabric over corners and curves; check the pattern doesn't end up upside down or on the wrong side. You can place cut-out shapes or motifs of fabric if you wish (the single-image method overleaf) but expect the edges to fray. 'This works if you are going for a shabby-chic feel, but I prefer a totally covered piece where the material overlaps, creating a continuous surface pattern,' says Amelia.

'Most paper and card has a grain just like wood does (handmade paper being an exception). When decoupaging large pieces of paper to wood or card, you will get the best results if the grains are running in the same direction. To check the grain direction of paper, bend it – it will be easier to fold along the grain.'

SARAH POUNDER, DESIGNER AND FOUNDER OF HOUSE OF ISMAY

houseofismay.com

'I use only vintage imagery, which I collect from vintage books and magazines. I always use the originals, because they have a great feel, but you could photocopy them.'

LISA TILLEY, FOUNDER OF U OLD BAG

uoldbag.com

The project

A FANCY PAIR OF SHOES

Making a pair of shoes from scratch is hardly feasible (for that you'll need a whole workshop of highly experienced craftspeople), but customising plain ones is an effective way to craft unique shoes you love.

HOW HARD IS IT TO DO?
It's fiddly, but not difficult.

HOW LONG DOES IT TAKE?
A weekend.

MATERIALS

1 **Leather shoes**

2 **Stamps**

3 **Waterproof découpage glue**

4 **Paintbrush**

5 **Needle/pin**

6 **Scissors**

7 **Sandpaper**

STEP 1
If you've got a pair of patent shoes, give them the once over with a piece of fine sandpaper to help the glue stick. Otherwise, just make sure they're clean and dry.

STEP 2
Organise your stamps before you start sticking, either by colours or pattern. You want approximately the same number and style of stamps to decorate each shoe.

STEP 3
Get the first stamp positioned correctly, then the rest is much easier. On your right shoe, hold the stamp in place with your left hand (as below), then use your right to drag the end of a pin along the crevice where the side of the shoe meets the heel. Cut along the line left by the pin. Cover the back of the stamp with découpage glue and stick in place.

STEP 4
The next stamp should line up with the first (for my shoes I overlapped the white edges so there was less white and more colour). Glue it as before. Should you need to wiggle it so it's in exactly the right place, do so using a wet, clean finger before it dries.

STEP 5
Keep adding stamps down the side of the shoe towards the toe, taking time to line them up before you stick.

STEP 6
Very soon you'll run into the rim of the shoe and wonder what to do. Stick to a simple rule: only glue the outside of the shoe. Leave the top of the stamps sticking up for now (don't fold them over the rim); we'll deal with these later.

STEP 7
Stop adding stamps when you've covered half of the toe (as below).

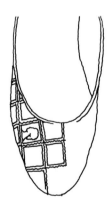

Now return to that first stamp you stuck on: add stamps to the left of it, working over the back, and part way down the other side. Here's your next obstacle: on the most curved points you're left with a peculiar, non-stamp-shaped space to fill. To tackle this, add stamps in the usual way until they just don't fit. Then, cut up your stamp into little pieces, and patchwork it together so the white edges line up with the existing white edges (don't fret if the Queen's head now looks like a Picasso).

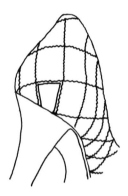

STEP 8
Soon the Queen's head will almost be on its side. Stop adding stamps at this point.

STEP 9
Start a new line of stamps, with the Queen's head the right way up.

Cover this side of the shoe as you did before, only stopping once you've covered the toe. (As in step 7, you'll need your patchworking skills to fill the odd-shaped spaces.

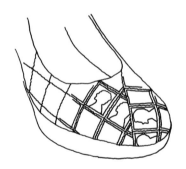

STEP 10
Coat the entire shoe in a layer of glue (take care not to get any on the heel or platform). Leave to dry, and repeat.

STEP 11
Finally, it's time to deal with the stamps sticking over the rim. Fold one over the rim, and use a pin to make a crease in it, where the outer meets the lining, as you did in step 3. Cut along the crease you just made, then stick the remaining stamp to the sliver of leather left. It won't stick easily, so hold it in place with your paintbrush while the glue dries a little. Repeat all the way around.

STEP 12
To finish, cover it with at least five layers of glue. When dry, add a few embellishments if you like. And remember, although waterproof découpage glue will protect from a light shower, heavy rain or jumping in puddles is to be avoided.

STEP 13
One shoe down, one more to go …

ALTERNATIVELY …
A more simple way to do this is to use the collage method and not worry about all the stamps lining up. Instead, stick them on at odd angles – the only steps you need to follow are steps 3 (to get the edges of the shoe neat), 11 (to get the rim neat) and 10 and 12 (to finish).

'MAKE
THE EVERYDAY
EXCITING!'

The extras

MAKE THE EVERYDAY EXCITING

Anything can be découpaged: picture frames, notebooks, placemats, jewellery boxes, leather bags, even telephones, guitars and Russian dolls. Take a look around your house and spot things you could give a makeover. Remember that anything rounded is more difficult to cover; to make it easier, I cut smaller pieces of paper than usual, and keep smoothing bumps down with a wet finger.

CREATE A FEATURE WALL

Instead of buying pricey wallpaper, try decoupaging a feature wall or ceiling with sheets of newspaper, maps, posters, photos or anything else you can find. Use wallpaper paste, not découpage glue, to stick the images down and, when dry, cover the entire wall with layers of clear varnish suitable for walls.

Or, I like the effect of the single image method. Either choose one standout image, or find loads that match (either by theme or by style). Blow up the pictures using a photocopier and carefully cut them out. Arrange them on the wall, using Blu-Tack to keep images in place, stand back, and decide whether the composition works (you could leave it up for a few days to decide if you like it enough) before sticking it down.

REWORK OLD JEWELLERY

This is a quick but effective method of upcycling old, naff jewellery. Cut out strips of paper and wrap them around a wooden or plastic chunky bangle, or cover large, flat beads with single pieces of paper. Round beads are fiddly to cover, but as shop-bought decorative beads can be so pricey, I think it's worth the effort (use your tweezers to position the tiny pieces of paper or fabric in the right place).

GLAMOURISE A CHEAP PIECE OF FURNITURE

I love that luxurious, decorative paper can turn something old and dull into something new that makes a real statement. The collage method is the most simple, but the all-in-one looks a little more refined. You needn't cover the entire piece of furniture: do the top of a dinner table, the insides of a set of bookshelves, the back of a glass cabinet or the front of a chest of drawers, for example. The rest could be painted to match or be left untouched. Because furniture generally needs to be more hard-wearing than accessories, finish off by applying a couple of extra coats of varnish.

CREATE A FANCY PIECE OF ARTWORK

Put anything in a frame and it looks great on the wall, right? Carefully cut a beautiful single image – a shoe, a flower, a piece of diamond jewellery from the pages of a magazine – and stick it on to a white piece of card and frame it. Or do a Warhol by sticking rows and rows of images cut to the same size on a piece of card or even a piece of wood (to hang the latter, use picture hooks). As you can't eat properly off découpaged plates, make the most of them by hanging a series of mismatched découpage plates on a single wall.

MAKE A DÉCOUPAGE MOSAIC

With a little careful planning, anything with can be mosaiced with paper (which is considerably cheaper, and less messy, than using proper mosaic tiles or chunks of ceramic). Sketch a design first, thinking about whether you want your paper 'tiles' to be square, circular, or another shape altogether (the beauty of this, unlike with traditional mosaic, is that you needn't stick to mini-squares because that's all that is available). Cut out your pieces and, before you stick, arrange on to the surface and check that you like it (use a blob of Blu-Tack to hold each piece in place if necessary). Once happy, I always take a photo that I can refer to while sticking it down. Cover tabletops, vases or similar.

How to avoid a craftastrophe

Craft can go very, very wrong. And in an age where your sad but amusing misfortunes are more likely to be splashed across YouTube than quietly forgotten, it's no surprise that the web has spawned a new generation of craft blogger who will track down photos of your epic fail and expose it to the world. I would hate for that to happen to you, so I asked the crafters behind those blogs to give us a lesson in good crafting ...

✄ *Recycling is not always a Good Thing*. 'Yes, old utensils make sounds when you clank them together. No, it is not pleasant to the ear and not everything that makes noise needs to be made into a wind chime,' says **Jen Farley** of Craigs Dump *(craigsdump.wordpress)*. Just because you can reuse something, it doesn't mean you should.

✄ *Think really carefully before you sell*. 'Anyone who feels their work is above judgment because they made it with their hands or it took a long time should not be selling to the public,' says **April Winchell** of Regretsy *(regretsy.com)*. 'You should be giving your crap to family members, who will only make fun of you when you're out of earshot.'

✄ *Find your inspiration anywhere, except in Lady Gaga*. 'Lady Gaga uses the most expensive, famous and skilled designers in the world, and she still winds up looking like a hot mess half the time,' says **Renee Nichols** of Craftastrophe *(craftastrophe. net)*. 'Trying to replicate her style with some felt and a hot-glue gun is a recipe for disaster.'

✄ *The ruler was invented for a reason*. 'Measuring isn't a craft-failer's strong suit,' says **Heather Mann** of Craft Fail *(craftfail.com)*. 'While you are planning, you must also take measurements and monitor progress as you go.' Think before you act is a pretty failsafe motto to craft by.

✄ *Ambition can be your downfall*. 'Stretch your abilities just a little at a time,' advises **Jen Yates**, founder of Cake Wrecks *(cakewrecks.com)*. 'And leave the life-sized recreation of your friend's favourite Fraggle for a time when you've already successfully made a Doozer or two.'

✄ *Mistakes can be telling*. 'If someone has mistaken your finished craft for trash, dirty laundry, or a kitty hairball, then you should probably just throw it away,' says Craigs Dump's Jen. Wise words indeed.

✄ *Chillax*. 'Taking yourself less seriously is the only way you can develop a critical eye for what you do,' says Regretsy's April.

✄ *Never, ever celebrate your womanhood*. 'Period-related craft is gross, period,' says Craftastrophe's Renee. 'No one wants to look at tampons pasted with red glitter or paintings made from menstrual blood. As the adage goes: keep it in your pants.'

Printing

*Two methods, one result: the ability to print
whatever you like on to whatever you want;
a T-shirt, a set of stationery, or even a roll of
wallpaper.*

The technique

MATERIALS

1 Something to print
Think something made of paper, card or fabric (and remember, whatever colour it is will affect how the paint looks when applied). Always test your print on scraps before cracking out the good stuff.

2 Printing ink
What type you choose depends on whether you're using a block or a screen, what you're printing on to and what finish you want. Some can be used on fabric and paper, others just on one surface. Look carefully at the label before you choose.

3 Iron
Some inks are set with heat.

FOR BLOCK PRINTING

1 Carving block
Rubber block or craft foam is easy to cut (to make a tiny stamp, an everyday pencil rubber does the job). Many professional printers prefer linoleum block because it's sturdy, so stamps last longer: it is, however, extremely difficult to carve.

2 Soft lead pencil

3 Lino cutter
A carving tool that comes with different-shaped interchangeable heads.

4 Paintbrush/ a brayer
A brayer (a special printing roller) is the best way to apply ink to your stamp. But, a paintbrush or mini roller is cheaper and essentially does the same job.

5 Greaseproof paper/ink plate
The latter is a posh printing tool. The former works OK too.

6 Barren
A luxury for the avid block printer which helps you apply pressure, or use a hardback book.

FOR SCREEN PRINTING

1 Screen-printing screen
A wooden frame covered with mesh.

2 A piece of plastic or card/a squeegee
Both tools help you drag paint across the screen.

3 Craft knife

4 Paper
Regular office paper is fine, as is newspaper.

BLOCK PRINTING

GETTING STARTED

This cheapo way of doing it isn't strictly block printing, but it can work almost as well when you stick to simple shapes (and don't mind wonky edges). Cut a shape from the side of a thick cardboard box or thick polystyrene, and you're done.

And now for how the pros do it…

Choose a design: it can be simple or detailed, depending on how much time and patience you have. Draw it on to the block freehand, or use one of the techniques on page 22 to transfer it. How difficult the next stage is depends on your material; rubber block and craft foam carve like butter, lino is like carving dense wood.

Cut away anything you don't want printed. Hold the tool like a pencil, or however it feels comfortable, and always – I mean always – carve away from your body. Place the block on a flat surface and keep it steady with your other hand, but never put your fingers in the line of the carve.

Carve slowly and carefully, applying only as much pressure as is needed; press too hard and you could slip and take out an unwanted chunk.

First, chisel around the image using the V-shaped head or the smallest one you have. Next, attempt the fiddly details, then take out the big chunks with the largest head (carve towards the edge of the block, not towards your nicely-cut pattern). Curves aren't always easy, but for a smoother line, hold the carving tool still and rotate the block instead (put a piece of paper under the block and it'll move more easily).

Are you happy with how it looks? Yes? Excellent. Get rid of the dust and pencil marks with water, and leave to dry.

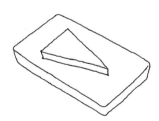

THE PRINTING

Should you have all the proper paraphernalia, squirt a dollop of ink on your ink plate and roll your brayer over it until it's evenly covered (it's ready when it makes a sticky, snapping sound). Then, simply roll the brayer over your carved-out block and you're prepared for printing.

I don't recommend forking out for fancy materials until you've fallen in love with this craft. So instead, lay out a piece of greaseproof paper, add a blob of ink, and use a paint roller, sponge or brush to add the ink to the block. Just make sure it's evenly covered and not too thick.

Press the block down, and lay something with a big, flat surface on top – a hardback book works brilliantly (or use a brayer, the 'official' tool for this job). Apply even pressure, then gently lift the block away from the paper or fabric. I'm sure it looks magnificent. You might be able to print again without re-applying another layer of ink, but that's for you to judge.

Effects to try

✀ *Shadowing:* once the ink is dry, take the same block and the same coloured ink and press it a couple of millimetres to the side of the original print.

✀ *Two-tone:* using the same block, but different-coloured paint, press the block over the pattern you've just printed. Don't worry about lining it up – the more skewed it appears, the more effective the look.

✀ *The two-block approach:* create two blocks that work together to create a single, two-coloured pattern. A basic example is a flower – make a petal block and a leaf block – but this could be done with any design.

TO FINISH

Leave your printed fabric or paper to dry. Check the instructions on your ink to see if you need to heat-set it with an iron.

COMMON PROBLEMS

My pattern isn't as crisp as I'd like. Are you keeping the block absolutely still on the surface? If so, check the block for fluffy edges and re-cut accordingly.

There's paint on my fabric where I didn't expect it to be. You must have got paint on the edges of your block. Be more careful when applying it next time.

SCREEN PRINTING

GETTING STARTED

Here's a crude method you could try, though not technically screen-printing, it has a similar effect, albeit without the super-crisp edges. Create a stencil using the paper-cutting advice on page 59, attach it to your fabric or paper using masking tape, and dab on fabric paint through the stencil with a sponge.

But now for the official technique …

Intricate designs are much easier for beginners to execute using screen rather than block printing: cut out a stencil using the paper-cutting rules on page 59 and you're ready to start printing. Your cut-out pattern must be no larger than the screen, and cut on a piece of paper no smaller than the screen.

THE PRINTING

Lay the material you want to print on a flat, sturdy surface (if you're printing a T-shirt or similar, insert a piece of card inside so the ink doesn't go through both layers). Position the stencil in place and the screen on top.

Do you remember your paper had to be bigger than the screen? That's because the only fabric or paper visible through the screen's mesh should be through your cut-out pattern: if the paper does not cover even a 5mm ($^1/_4$in) strip down one side, that could accidentally get inked, too.

Now is not the time for clumsiness. The paper and screen must stay in exactly the same place to avoid messy edges. With one hand, hold the screen: with the other take a spoon of ink and blob it across the top of the mesh.

Hold the squeegee or piece of thick cardboard at 45 degrees above the line of ink and drag it down firmly, bringing the paint over the stencil. Carefully lift the screen up when you're done.

FINISHING OFF

You can see that the paper stencil has stuck to the screen, right? Should you want to make another print using that stencil, do it again quickly. Otherwise, take it off before the ink dries, and wash the screen with water and a scrubbing brush. Leave the screen and newly printed fabric or paper to dry naturally (and remember to heat-set it with an iron if the instructions say so).

COMMON PROBLEMS

The colour isn't as intense as I'd like it to be. After dragging the ink down, push the remainder back up the screen, over the stencil, adding another layer.

My design isn't very crisp. The screen must have moved while you inked. Get a friend to hold it next time, or consider using a screen with a higher count of mesh. If you really like this screen-printing thing, invest in different meshes, which offer different degrees of detail.

CUSTHOM DESIGN
ON CREATING A SMART BLOCK-PRINT PATTERN
DESIGN DUO NATHAN PHILPOTT AND JEMMA OOI
CREATE SOME OF THE MOST SLEEK AND CONTEMPORARY
WALLPAPERS AND PRINTS AROUND (WHICH IS WHY THEY'VE
WORKED WITH THE LIKES OF JOHN LEWIS, BODEN AND
ANTHROPOLOGIE). *custhom.co.uk*

BE SMART WITH YOUR SHAPES
'Straight edges with corners are a lot simpler to start with,' they say. 'We find triangles work really well and are very versatile.'

DON'T GET STUCK IN THE DETAIL
'Larger, bolder patterns are much easier to get looking professional,' they advise. Aim for thicker lines and large shapes if you're new to block printing, because if you accidentally cut away too much, there's no going back.

EXPERIMENT BEFORE YOU PRINT
Unless you're just printing a single image on to a piece of paper, you must consider how your block will look when it's repeated over and over again. 'The easiest way to do this is to photocopy a drawing of your block design several times, then lay it out in different combinations.'

BUILD UP THE PATTERN
'Sometimes the simplest of shapes make the most exciting compositions. Randomly printing and changing the direction of the block always work well,' they recommend. Print the block as you would see a brick wall, so the motifs are not all in regimented straight lines, or make larger shapes out of simple shapes printed next to one and other.

INSIDER TRICKS

'Mix your own individual ink colours in plastic food-storage tubs; the airtight lid means they'll last for ages. Use cheap plastic spatulas to mix the ink, and scrape off excess ink from the screen after you've printed to reduce waste.'

MEGAN PRICE, CREATOR OF PRINTED GOODS LABEL MR PS

mr–ps.co.uk

LEE MAY FOSTER-WILSON

ON MAKING A MULTICOLOURED SCREEN PRINT
SCREEN PRINTER LEE MAY IS THE CREATOR OF THE
FANTASTICAL WORLD OF 'BONBI FOREST', AND HER
SCARVES, TEES, CARDS AND ACCESSORIES HAVE BEEN
RECOMMENDED BY THE LIKES OF *VOGUE*, *GRAZIA*
AND *ELLE*. *bonbiforest.com*

CUT YOUR STENCIL

Bear in mind that each colour in your design needs a separate stencil, so if you are a beginner, don't make the design too complicated. If you want a flower, for example, you need to do a stencil for the stem (green), petals (pink) and centre (yellow). The easiest way to do this is to photocopy your original drawing three times: on the first stencil cut out just the stem, on the second, the petals, and on the third, the centre.

PRINT IN THE RIGHT ORDER

Print the colours that depict the background first (the stem). Then, when you print the foreground colours, you get a better illusion of them being in front or on top. Wait for each layer of paint to dry before adding the next colour.

GET IT LINED UP

Once you've printed the first colour, put the second stencil in position; try to align it as best you can using your knowledge of the design and what you can see.

IT DOESN'T MATTER IF YOUR SHAPES OVERLAP

I think it adds to the hand-printed look and makes each print individual and unique. Different printing inks behave differently when colours overlap: some will sit on top of each other without the lower colours showing through; others will be more transparent and you will get a tertiary colour effect. The best thing to do is experiment with designs and inks and learn each time you do it.

'To get the best results, make sure the paper/fabric you're printing on to fits the job. Something with a smooth surface should take the ink well. Rougher surfaces will need lots more pulls of the squeegee to get a good coating and won't take fine detail as well.'

SAM WINGATE, THE TEXTILE DESIGNER BEHIND
THE MR WINGATE LABEL

wingateprint.com

'A cheap way of learning to block print is to use the foam backing from ready-made pizzas. You can draw directly into this with a pencil to make indentations and create your printing block.'

GILLIAN ELAM, ONE-THIRD OF CRAFT COLLECTIVE
THE SEASIDE SISTERS

seasidesisters.co.uk

The project

A PERSONALISED, PRINTED SCARF

Because every outfit looks more chic when you've got a pretty little scarf tied around your neck.

HOW HARD IS IT TO DO?
Once you've made the block it's plain sailing.

HOW LONG DOES IT TAKE?
It depends how big your scarf is.

MATERIALS

1. **Block-printing equipment and paint** (SEE PAGE 54)

2. **Fabric**

3. **Bin bag**

4. **Scissors**

5. **Needle**

6. **All-purpose thread**

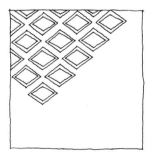

STEP 1
Choose your fabric. Muslin or cheesecloth will make a floaty, lightweight scarf, but the paint will seep through so you mustn't move the fabric while printing (any shift at all will cause it to smudge). Or, use a thicker cotton; the paint won't seep through but it will make your scarf stiffer.

STEP 2
Design and carve your block. Any shape goes, but the smaller it is, the longer it will take to cover the whole piece of fabric with prints. If you fancy a two-colour pattern, carve two identical shapes from the one block – one can be covered in one colour, the other in another. You like the pattern I created? Use the template on page 218 to carve two diamond shapes; when you're done, cut the block along the dashed line: this means you just line the edge of the block up with the diamond you just printed, and you can be sure the shapes will all be evenly spaced. Experiment on scrap fabric first to get confident with your block.

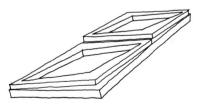

STEP 3
Cut your fabric to the size you want your scarf to be, adding 2cm (³/₄in) seams the whole way around (most neck scarves are 60cm x 60cm/24in x 24in, so cut 64cm x 64cm/26in x 26in). Cover a flat, steady surface with a bin bag (to protect it from seeping-through paint), and lay your fabric on top. Take it slowly. Should you make a mistake near the beginning, you can afford to start again; if you're almost finished, you're better off embracing the flaw than scrapping an entire project.

STEP 4
Once printed, carefully peel the fabric off the bin bag and leave it to dry according to the instructions on the paint packet. (I recommend hanging it up with clothes pegs.) When it's dry, it's time to stitch.

STEP 5
Lay your newly printed fabric right-side down. Fold one edge over 1cm (¹/₂in), then 1cm (¹/₂in) again, to create a neat seam: pin in place and repeat for the other three sides (make sure the corners are neatly folded). Sew all the way around with a backstitch or sewing machine.

STEP 6
If you wish, add extra embellishments around the edge, such as sequins or tassels.

The extras

THE OBVIOUS CANDIDATES

Cushions, canvas bags, T-shirts, tea towels, purses, bunting, birthday cards … anything you usually see printed and sold in shops can be made at home now. Go for simple shapes, go for something intricate; whatever takes your fancy. I especially like to print birthday cards for men, as I can never find decent ones in the shops.

MAKE ART WITHOUT HAVING TO PAINT

Take your time and create one super-detailed print to display proudly in a frame. You could reproduce a limited-edition run for friends and family (don't forget to number them 1 of 20, 2 of 20 and so on, like proper artists do). It could be a simplified version of the house you grew up in, your surname in decorative lettering or an old family saying. Think carefully about the frame (you'd be a fool to whack it in any old thing because the frame maketh the print): anything highly detailed should go in something plain, while anything very simple can afford to be framed ornately.

BECOME A PATTERN DESIGNER

Now you're well versed in two methods of printing, there's no need to fret about finding that perfect fabric; just print your own. A metre of cheap cotton and a few ideas are all you need. (And, personalised fabric means those easy-to-make purses, cushions, T-shirts and canvas bags become much more thoughtful gifts). Wrapping paper can be printed, too (I like to use cheap rolls of brown paper from the Post Office as my base, and I always print on the non-shiny side). If you want to take on something bigger, what about printing your own wallpaper? If starting from scratch leaves you feeling nervous, add extra detail to already-printed fabric, paper or wallpaper (anything with spots or stripes on makes a great base).

CREATE A PERSONALISED STAMP

A gift for the person who has everything. Carve someone's name, initials or favourite little shape into a mini block, and give it to them with a pad of their favourite colour of ink. Or, if you're feeling rather more selfish, create one for yourself. How about a 'handmade by me' to stamp on the back of anything you've made? Just remember to carve any words back to front.

SLEEP SWEETLY (AND CHEAPLY)

A beautiful duvet cover is one of those items that costs a fair bit (and in a match between a new pair of shoes and something new to cover your bed, you know the former will win every time). But it is essential, and a bad one can ruin the perfectly crafted look of your bedroom, so this is one of those times when making one from scratch is a good idea.

To make a duvet cover, patchwork three long pieces of fabric together to make the top, and three to make the bottom (use the measurements from your old duvet cover, and remember to allow for extra width for the seams; see the tutorial on page 21).* Hem one short side on both pieces.

Now to print the top with whatever design you like (I fancy something Fair Isle-inspired). Pin the printed (and dry) top sheet to the bottom sheet, right sides facing, and stitch securely around the two long edges and the short edge you left unhemmed. Sew press studs along the hemmed, open edge, and you're ready for a good night's sleep.

ALTERNATIVELY ...
Buy super-wide sheeting fabric, available from good fabric shops.

Any problem solved

The internet really is the best thing ever invented. But if you're not interested in cat videos and an endless supply of porn, you might like to put the web to good use for all your crafting dilemmas. Allow the UK's best craft journalists to be your guide.

THE PROBLEM: I'M UNINSPIRED
You've got a box full of beautiful materials, but no idea what to use them for.

The solution

In theory you've got the entire web to help fire your imagination, but rather than trawl through Google listings, check out a few of these sites first. Flickr is the place to go to 'gain access to gazillions of projects, inspiration and ideas quickly', says **Jen Fox-Proverbs**, publisher of *CrossStitcher (themakingspot.com)*. 'Seeing photographs from non-crafters is an amazing opportunity for creative growth.'

Going down the visual route is clearly your best bet, as **Jane Toft**, editor of *Mollie Makes*, adds *(molliemakes. themakingspot.com)*: 'It's always worth a visit to Pinterest [the online pinboard where users can easily share images they love]. I have built up a selection of boards that I follow, so I can guarantee I have at least 20 pairs of very design-savvy eyes pinning great things from around the web.' And although this is not its main function, Etsy.com and other handmade marketplaces can fulfil a similar role. 'I often go on to those sites just to browse and see what's out there,' says **Sian Hamilton** of *Making* magazine *(makingmagazine.com)*. (For the sake of decency, though, don't rip off someone else's design and pass it off as your own. That's just not on.)

My advice

Me, I'm all about the blogs; trust me, there are hundreds you'll want to follow. I paste links to all my favourite ones in my RSS reader so I never miss any posts (or forget the link).

THE PROBLEM: I'M STUCK

Your thread/paper/fabric/glue won't stay/cut/twisted/stuck. What the hell do you do?

The solution

Head to YouTube, suggests **Harriet de Winton** and **Ros Marshall**, editors of *Cloth* magazine *(clothmagazine.co.uk)*. 'You're going to learn faster if someone sits next to you and shows you, but when you don't have that, video is the next best thing.' No matter how peculiar your problem is, there's sure to be the explanatory film you need on there (I must warn you that many of them are pretty tedious, but if you can sit through them, you'll be a better crafter for it).

Craft forums are a brilliant source of advice too, says *Making*'s Sian. 'When you're struggling to make something work, the first place I would turn is a forum.' Search for existing conversations on that topic, or ask a question and watch the advice come flooding in. *Ravelry.com* is the most notorious (but is only for knitters), while the likes of *Craftster.org* and *CutOutAndKeep.net* deal with all crafts.

My advice

When I'm stuck, I ask my Twitter followers; they always send me the most incredible tricks and links. To get a range of advice you need to be followed by a number of crafters; get more followers by following them first, tweeting great craft advice, links or pictures yourself, and adding your love of craft to your bio.

THE PROBLEM: I'M A LONE CRAFTER

You love to make, but your mates don't (they even give you strange looks when you whip out your embroidery on the bus. Tsk.). When even the promise of cupcakes and clothes won't get them to a craft fair, you need to take some action.

The solution

Pay Twitter a visit, says *Mollie Makes*' Jane. 'You get to be involved with a funny and supportive bunch of like-minded people. These people are part of a worldwide community that make and appreciate beautiful and quirky things.' They tweet, you reply, and over time you'll find relationships form. Just because you don't know them in real life, it doesn't make it odd, no matter what the Twitter-haters say. (I've found plenty of craft-loving friends on Twitter, and none of them have been crazy yet.)

If you can't face Twitter, however, *Making*'s Sian has a suggestion. 'Forums play a big part in creating a strong craft community. When I worked from home I felt quite cut off and forums were a godsend, knowing there were other people out there interested in the same thing as me.'

My advice

Maybe your real-life friends don't like craft because they don't know enough about it. In an attempt to convert my mates, I post the occasional slice of craft on Facebook – amusing links, pretty handmade dresses – things that I know non-crafters will enjoy. I like to think it's working …

THE PROBLEM: I'M BRILLIANT (BUT NO ONE KNOWS IT)

You might have faith in your witty and insightful blog, or your well-designed and hand-stitched purses, but if no one stumbles upon them, how are you going to become the next big craft thing?

The solution

Embrace Twitter, say the *Cloth* editors. 'Quite often our magazine contributors come from people we follow and hear about on Twitter. We found one girl like this and her work ended up on the front cover.' Pretty impressive. *Mollie Makes*' Jane uses this route, too. 'We crowd-source on Twitter for upcoming features and ask for recommendations for blogs and companies to follow up.'

Even hanging around on Facebook can get you noticed. 'I'm amazed by how quickly some people can become regular voices on the magazine's fan page,' says *CrossStitcher*'s Jen. 'We start taking real interest in what they say and how other visitors to the page react to them. Keep up to date with what's happening and maintain a presence,' she advises, 'because you never know what opportunities will arise.'

Follow these magazines, as well as fashion and interiors glossies, and don't be afraid to say hello. Remember, you don't need a press release to get in the press anymore.

My advice

Get yourself a website. You can't pack a proper punch in 140 characters, so use one of the free sites (Wordpress, Blogger, Tumbler, etc.) to tell everyone who you are and what you do. Blog about craft-in-progress to get readers excited about your work, and share the link wherever you can.

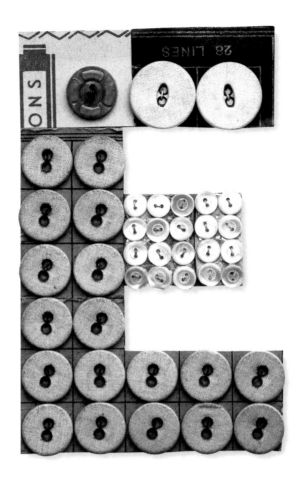

Encrusting

While some of us covet things drenched in crystals, others prefer a tasteful splash of sparkle instead. Once you've mastered the art of encrusting with beads, sequins and buttons, you're in control of the bling.

The technique

MATERIALS

1 Embellishments
Beads and buttons can be massive or miniscule and can be made from ceramics, glass, plastic, metal and more. Sequins come flat or with facets, and gems can be found in all shapes and sizes.

2 Needle
As long as it has a sharp point and fits through the centre of your bead or sequin, it'll work perfectly.

3 Glue
What you use depends on what you're sticking, and what it's being stuck to.

4 Strong cotton thread

5 Sewing scissors

6 Embroidery hoop

GETTING STARTED

If you're attaching more than five embellishments to a piece of fabric, don't use the same piece of thread to stitch them all on; add a few at a time. Then, if you're unlucky enough to have the thread snap, it won't ruin all of your hard work. Use an embroidery hoop if you have one, as sewing on embellishments is easier if the fabric is taut.

BUTTONS
The instructions for sewing on buttons can be found on page 19. To attach decorative buttons, sew on without the matchstick, so it lies flat on the fabric. Make a feature of the stitches by choosing a thread that clashes with the colour of the button. Or, if you have a four-button hole, stitch diagonally across holes to form a standard cross, or sew across different holes to create a square, two lines or an arrow. It's all in the details.

SEQUINS

A single sequin can be sewn on in two ways. Push the needle through the central hole, and make one stitch over the sequin. Repeat this once or twice, and secure the thread. Alternatively, push the needle through the hole and thread on a small bead. Take the needle back down through the hole, and the bead will rest on top, holding it in place. Secure the thread.

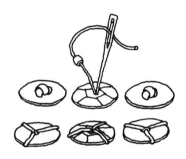

BEADS

To attach a single bead, push the needle through the fabric, thread the bead on, then push the needle back down. Use your finger or thumb to hold it in place, and repeat once or twice before you secure the thread.

Rows of beads are best sewn on in groups (a technique called 'couching'). Push the needle up through the fabric and thread on a few beads. Push the needle back into the fabric so the beads sit nicely on top. To keep them all in place, sew a tiny stitch over the original thread between each bead, and secure the thread.

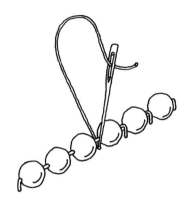

STICKY STUFF

When you want to encrust anything that's not fabric, it's time to crack out the glue. Always check the label to ensure it's right for the surfaces you're sticking together, but this guide covers the basics.

✄ *PVA or glue stick* is usually useless. Use this and your embellishments will fall off.

✄ *Superglue or a hot-glue gun* will both normally stick card, wood, metal, fabric, leather, ceramics and some plastics. Some types will stick glass, others won't.

✄ *Epoxy glue* comes to the rescue when you need something of industrial strength; it can stick wood, glass, stone and some types of plastic.

Stick on individual gems by applying glue to the back of each (a tube of glue with a nozzle is easiest to control), then press it on to the surface. To cover a large area, cover sections with a thin layer of glue, then position the embellishments in place (tweezers come in handy to avoid sticky fingers). Some glues need to become tacky before you press two surfaces together, while others need to be held together for a period of time to ensure they stick.

FINISHING OFF

Take care when washing anything that has been encrusted; if you have the time and inclination, hand washing will keep clothes looking sparkling. A duster, rather than a damp cloth, is best for cleaning embellished homewares.

COMMON MISTAKES

My beads shatter when I try to thread them. Your needle is too thick. Try a thinner one, and be more gentle.

My embellishments fall off once the glue has dried. You're using the wrong glue. Check the label to ensure you've got the right stuff.

The masterclass

J MASKREY
ON KEEPING CRYSTALS STYLISH

FROM BJÖRK TO BRITNEY, DEBBIE HARRY TO RIHANNA, SOME OF THE WORLD'S MOST RECOGNISABLE NAMES HAVE WORN THIS DESIGNER'S CRYSTAL-ENCRUSTED CLOTHES AND ACCESSORIES. *jmaskrey.com*

BE INSPIRED BY THE CLASSICS

'I do a lot of research before I start work on a collection. I look at old movie stars, Cartier jewellery, and go to exhibitions,' J explains. It's also worth taking a stroll around antique fairs and flicking through picture books of fine jewellery collections to see how the great designers made encrusting work.

DESIGN FOR YOUR FANTASY ALTER EGO

'Normally a collection is based around some form of a girl. I invent a character and create the kind of things she would wear. It really helps because you can go as far as you want to.' Maybe you wouldn't wear a crystal-covered cuff, but your alter ego might …

PREPARE, PREPARE, PREPARE

'Some people just throw crystals on, and it doesn't always look great.' But not J. 'I will do a placement and go back and change it, and change it and change it until it's perfect.' Arrange your pieces, but don't sew or glue them on straight away; come back a few hours, or days, later to check you still love the arrangement. Far better to scrap an entire design before attaching it than hate it a week after making it.

BE ADVENTUROUS

Working with classic white crystals seems like the obvious way to keep something looking stylish. But not always, warns J. 'Sometimes when you use classic tones you can look like an old lady. You want to put in a splash of clash to make it a little more modern, a bit more youthful, a bit more fresh.' Team gold stones with grey, or dark hues with acid brights.

START SIMPLE

'Some people jump in and they do a brilliant job. They have a taste for crystals and they make it work. Other people can end up making a mess.' So, she advises people to 'Start with a smaller element and then build on it. Don't go in at the deep end and say "I'm going to cover a whole dress with crystals". Think about how to make something very simple and very effective and very beautiful.'

INSIDER TRICKS

'I work in an intuitive way with the embellishments. I never plan exactly where to stitch the beads or sequins, as I would rather judge the development of the design as I'm going along.'

CHARLOTTE LIDDLE, TEXTILE ARTIST

charlotteliddle.co.uk

LAURA WALKER

ON DIY BUTTONS

I THINK WE'D ALL AGREE THAT LAURA HAS ONE OF THE BEST
JOBS IN THE WORLD: DESIGNING AND MAKING BEAUTIFUL
BUTTONS THAT ARE SOLD IN BOUTIQUES ACROSS THE UK.
laura–walker.co.uk

MAKE YOUR BASE

Roll a piece of Fimo (oven-hardening modelling clay)
flat until it's the thickness you want (2–5mm is best).
Cut your buttons out with a small cookie cutter, or
similar. Smooth the edges with your fingers, and use
something like a cocktail stick to poke two holes in
the middle.

ADDING THE DETAIL

Find something made of metal, plastic or glass which
has an interesting texture or pattern – the end of a
decorative teaspoon, an old vintage button or a piece of
jewellery, for example. Clean it (so things like fluff and
tiny hairs don't contaminate the button) and carefully
press it into the Fimo. Be especially careful with white
stuff, as it is less forgiving if you don't get off all the
dirt. Put the buttons on a baking tray and bake in the
oven, as per the instructions on the packet.

THE FINISHING TOUCHES

Once baked and cooled, sand any rough edges with
fine sandpaper or a nail file, then varnish with two
coats of water-based varnish. Alternatively, add an
antique effect: before you varnish, cover the buttons
in a contrasting colour of acrylic paint and, once dry,
rub some of the raised areas and the edges with fine
sandpaper or a nail file.

'Choose buttons that add something
to the fabric and don't blend in too
much; otherwise your hard work
could go unnoticed.'

EMMA TOFT, DESIGNER

toftymakes.com

'Always mix and match when
encrusting; the finished item will look
less contrived if it's made from a
mix of embellishments. For example,
a heart shape made out of crystals
on the side of a vase could verge on
tacky; a linen cushion with a petal
shape made of buttons, neon threads

and one sequin in the centre would
look more tasteful.'

WILL TAYLOR, INTERIORS BLOGGER
AND PROP STYLIST

brightbazaar.blogspot.com

The project

AN ENCRUSTED BELT

Once you've mastered this,
you can accessorise even the most
hard-to-match outfit.

HOW HARD IS IT TO DO?
If you can sew, you can make this.

HOW LONG DOES IT TAKE?
An intricate design? A couple of
evenings. Something more simple?
Your Saturday afternoon.

MATERIALS

1 **Thick elastic**

   I USED 8CM/3IN WIDE ELASTIC
   BECAUSE I LIKE THICK BELTS, BUT IF
   YOU WANT SOMETHING MORE DELICATE,
   GO FOR 4CM/1½IN OR 6CM/2IN WIDE)

2 **Beads**

3 **Belt clasp**

4 **Thick fabric**

   I USED A LINEN. DON'T USE ANYTHING STRETCHY
   LIKE FELT – IT NEEDS TO BE STURDY. IT CAN MATCH
   THE COLOUR OF YOUR ELASTIC, OR NOT

5 **Needle**

6 **Black thread**

7 **White thread**

8 **Scissors**

9 **Embroidery hoop**

10 **Iron**

STEP 1
This really is far easier to do than it
looks: you add beads to two pieces
of thick fabric, then sew a piece
to each end of the thick elastic.
Take your fabric and mark out a
rectangle that is 15cm (6in) long,
and the height of your elastic (to
do this, I pinned my elastic to the
black fabric and sewed long tacking
stitches around it in white thread.
You could use tailor's chalk, too).
Don't cut anything out just yet.

STEP 2
Add 4cm (1½in) to the top and
bottom edge of this fabric rectangle
(or 3cm/1in if your elastic is
6cm/2in wide; 2cm/¾in if it's
4cm/1½in). Add 2cm/¾in to the
left short edge, and 17cm/7in to
the right short edge (no matter
how wide the elastic is). Cut it out.
You will be left with a 16cm/7in
high, 34cm/14in long rectangle
which has a small rectangle marked
out inside (smaller if you're using
thinner elastic). Give it a good iron.
This piece of fabric will eventually
make one side of the front of
your belt.

STEP 3
Decide on your pattern: simple,
intricate, tiny glass beads, giant
sequins – anything goes. It can
be symmetrical with the other
side that you'll make later, or not.

Just make sure you only encrust inside the marked-out rectangle (about 1mm from the edge), and leave at least 5cm (2in) free of embellishments at the far left. Put the thick fabric in an embroidery hoop and encrust your little heart out.

STEP 4
You're done? Excellent! Remove the embroidery hoop. Lay your fabric on a flat surface, beads facing down. Fold the left, short side of the fabric over 2cm (³/4in) and iron the crease to hold it in place. Do the same at the right, short side. Now fold the long, top edge to the middle, and iron (being very careful not to iron over the beads, of course). Fold the long, bottom edge up to the middle, and iron again. (The fabric is now 8cm (3in) high and 30cm (12in) long, or marginally smaller if using thinner elastic – see step 2.)

STEP 5
Fold this long strip in half (the fold line should be exactly where your beads start. This piece is now 8cm (3in) high and 15cm (6in) long.

STEP 6
Poke about 3–4cm (1–1¹/4in) of the elastic in between the two layers of thick fabric. Does the fabric lie almost flush to the top of the elastic? Yes? Great. Pin it and sew it in place using four or five lines of strong backstitch, about 1mm apart. (This must be secure, else you risk it coming apart after a particularly large meal. Not something I'd wish on anyone.)

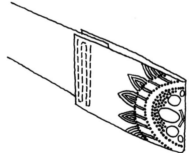

STEP 7
Oversew the top and bottom edge of the black fabric neatly to tidy up the edges. Put the half-finished belt up to your waist, and work out how long the elastic needs to be (remember, 3–4cm (1–1¹/4in) needs to be poked inside the front piece at the other end). Cut the elastic to size.

STEP 8
Repeat steps 1–7 to make the second front piece. (Remember, if you want your encrusted pattern to be symmetrical, you need to flip everything, so that the marked-out rectangles sits on the right side of the fabric.)

STEP 9
To finish, securely (very securely – again, think of those big dinners) sew each side of your belt clasp to the underside of each front piece, as you would a hook and eye (see page 20). You can sew it so the little clasp only just pokes out and is essentially invisible when you're wearing it, or you can make a feature of it and sew the clasp closer to the edge; it depends on your taste, and how fancy your clasp is.

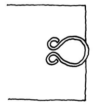

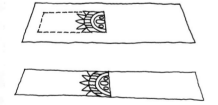

'DESIGN FOR YOUR FANTASY ALTER EGO'

The extras

COUTURE ENCRUSTING

It sounds easy enough: whack a few bits and bobs on to a T-shirt or bag and it'll look like something from London Fashion Week. But not so; getting this encrusting business right requires a lot of thought. (Get it wrong and you'll look like you were attacked by a children's craft club.) Here's a few guidelines I stick to in order to avoid such pitfalls.

✄ *Work with the logo or design already there.* Cover the whole thing in embellishments (it's great if you have a letter or word on the front of a T-shirt), or follow the outline.

✄ *Use the shape of the garment as your guide.* Cover the cuffs or the collar of a top, stitch a line of beads down a seam or around the waistband or neckline, or cover the straps (do this to a plain ballgown and it can look incredible. Check out how couture dresses are embellished to keep it sophisticated). Add beading around the edge of a clutch bag or cover the entire flap of a satchel.

✄ *Let the pattern help you.* Sew sequins down every other stripe or on every other polka dot. You needn't cover an entire garment, just do a patch or cover a pocket.

GLAM UP A LAST-MINUTE GIFT

You know how it works: you've forgotten a birthday, so you have to pop out at the last minute to buy a generic bottle of wine/ pot of nail varnish/supermarket birthday card. But, have a handy stash of gems to hand and you can transform anything into a special, limited-edition, encrusted version. A memory stick entirely covered in miniature crystals becomes a perfectly acceptable present. A bog-standard bottle of fizz with crystals cascading down the side becomes something they'll save for a special occasion. (High-end cosmetic brands do it all the time: a lipstick/nail varnish/eye-shadow palette with a few sparkles on the lid sparks a surge in demand for an otherwise general product.) Or, add a few sparkles to a plain shop-bought card to make it look far more extravagant.

HOME IS WHERE THE SPARKLE IS

Look around: you've got an entire room/flat/house full of things that might look better with a touch of beading or bling. Find the right glue and pretty much anything can be encrusted: a plain picture frame, the lid of a jewellery box … the list is endless. Be very careful, though – embellish a few small things in one room (a set of cushions) or go for one large piece (the frame of a large mirror) – anything more and you're in gangster-wives territory (if you use gems) or in danger of looking too 'crafty' (if you go for buttons). Stay stylish by mixing sparkle, beads and buttons with classic shapes (a Victorian lamp base) and classic patterns (a William Morris-inspired fabric). And, if you're concerned about getting it wrong or the piece looking too folksy, scout out inspiration from interiors' blogs for ideas that work.

PUT YOUR BEST FOOT FORWARD

Even the girl who wears nothing but neutrals and black can't resist a sparkly shoe. Encrust the heel or stitch or glue a cluster to the front of them (it's easier to sew a few of them on to a small piece of felt and then attach that). Add gems or pretty buttons to straps (I recommend sewing with a leather needle) or on to the thongs of flip-flops (glue is best; if you stitch, the thread could rub). And if you're feeling brave (and have a day to kill), you could stitch sequins all over your Converse or cover a pair of cheap leather heels entirely with crystals.

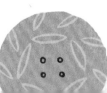

The F word

It might seem peculiar that a generation of thoroughly modern women have embraced craft; a very traditional, very domestic hobby that their mothers fought hard to shed. So are we unravelling fifty years of feminism by cracking out our needle and thread? Debbie Stoller, co-founder and editor-in-chief of US magazine *BUST*, and the author of the *Stitch'n'Bitch* series of knitting and crocheting books (*knithappens.com*) believes that is definitely NOT the case.

'A new generation of feminists think about craft very differently. Rather than the old approach – to reject bluntly things like fashion, beauty and craft – in the late 1980s and early 1990s we started to look at why these things had been abandoned, and whether we could reclaim them in some way. We were inspired by gay rights activists and Riot Grrl – the underground feminist punk movement – who embraced rather than fought words like "queer" and "girl", and recast them as something more positive. Women in the 1960s and 1970s had turned away from craft because they felt they had been restricted to sewing and knitting at the expense of all the other things they wanted to do. And because their efforts were not valued by the culture at large, they considered any handmade effort to be a waste of time (Germaine Greer has been much quoted as saying 'women have frittered their lives away stitching things for which there is no demand').

'We disagree. There is nothing more frivolous about making something than there is about playing some form of sport. But because craft is traditionally something that women have done, it's undervalued, because women have always been undervalued. So, thirty years later, we realised that by rejecting craft we were doing exactly what culture had always done: we were failing to appreciate work done by women.

'By the late 1990s, feminists had worked through fashion and beauty – picked the bits we liked, found different ways of doing the stuff we didn't – and started to think more seriously about craft and domestic work. The magazine I edit, *BUST*, started running a craft column, young feminists like Jean Railla began writing about craft on the web, and a couple of years later I was asked to write a book about knitting. Wider society was rethinking global corporate culture, too, straying away from disposable goods, and it also happened that, at the time, big chunky knits were in fashion and made people think: "I could probably make that." A number of things had come together to make it the right time for a big craft revival for women, and many men, too.

'A decade on, I think we've accomplished what we wanted. People have much more respect and admiration for what goes into these crafts. And as a result I think people are starting to put a higher value on centuries' worth of women's work, too.

'We're not quite there – the culture has shifted a lot in the last ten years, but the whole DIY movement hasn't quite spread out into the mainstream yet, nor lost all connotations about being something women do that can be celebrated. I don't think Hillary Clinton would be photographed knitting in the way Obama is frequently photographed playing sport, for example, but I think there will be a time when world leaders, male or female, could be.'

THE MARTHA EFFECT

'There are still a number of feminists who don't realise that this shift has occurred and who still believe craft ties women to the home, which is a shame. And I find it interesting that some criticise the likes of Martha Stewart (the US super crafter) for being unfeminist. That, somehow, showing women how to make everything from scratch means she's saying women *have* to make everything from scratch, no matter if they also have a career and family to look after. I don't see why women feel pressurised by this. I don't see men reading *Sports Illustrated* magazine and saying, "Oh my God, I'm supposed to play football and basketball and like to ski as well as having a career and family and social life.'

'Actually, I happen to think that Martha Stewart is one of our great feminist figures. In the past when magazines and shows about craft, cooking and cleaning were aimed at women, it was sold as something you should to do please your husband and children. But with Martha, there's never any mention of a husband or kids. It's about doing these things for your own pleasure, to enrich your own life.'

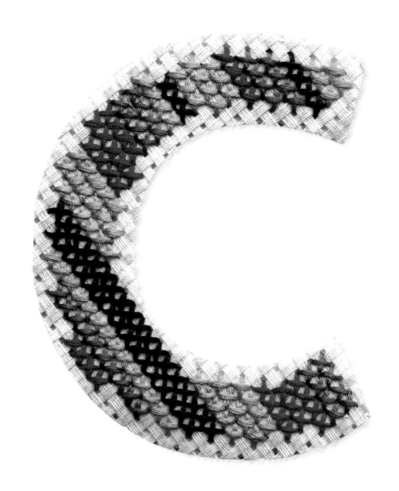

Cross stitching

Sewing doesn't get easier than this. Learn one simple-to-sew stitch and you can create the most detailed pattern you like. And these days, there are patterns for pretty much everything, from Banksy street art to Kate Middleton's face (yes, really).

The technique

MATERIALS

1 Tapestry needle
This has a blunt tip (so as not to damage the fabric) and a large eye (for easy threading).

2 Embroidery thread
Use three strands.

3 Aida
This is the most common cross-stitch fabric, covered in regularly-spaced holes (known as 'block weave') for easy stitching. Aida comes in different 'thread counts': the higher the count, the closer the holes, so the smaller your stitches will be (count 14 is typical for most projects). Or, use other fabrics with an even weave – linen or hessian, for example.

4 Embroidery hoop

5 Sewing scissors

SEWING A CROSS STITCH

Poke your needle up through the bottom-left hole and down through the top-right hole, to make a diagonal stitch. Then bring the needle up through the top-left hole and down through the bottom-right hole and – voila! – you have your first cross stitch.

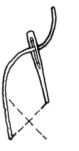 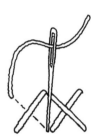

A simple way to do a whole row of stitches is to sew all the left-hand slants first, then go back and complete the right-hand slants.

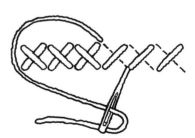

SEWING A HALF CROSS STITCH

When a picture calls for a nice slanted edge you'll need to execute a part or half cross stitch. Make the first diagonal stitch, as above, then poke the second through the middle of the fabric, rather than through the opposite top hole.

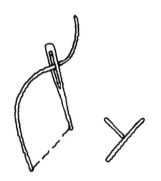

HOW TO FOLLOW A CHART

It's not as difficult as it looks, I promise. The symbols on the chart tell you where to put which stitch, and what colour thread you should use to make it. DMC, Anchor and Madeira are popular brands of thread, and the words and numbers in the key usually refer to specific colours in each of these brands.

Cut a piece of aida at least 2cm (³/₄in) larger on each side than the pattern requires (think about what you'll be doing with it when you've finished – framing it, turning it into a cushion or otherwise) and secure it in your embroidery hoop.

Start in the corner and stitch all of one colour. Be sure to count spaces between stitches properly – put one stitch wrong and the whole thing will be off. Then do all of the second colour, and so on. If a pattern is especially large, you might find it easier to complete sections at a time.

COMMON PROBLEMS

I put a cross stitch in the wrong square. What to do depends on how far into the pattern you are when you notice. If it's straight away, use your needle to unpick the offending stitch: no harm done. If you made the mistake ages ago, think about how much it'll affect the pattern if you leave it. Does it ruin the design? If not, brilliant. If so, I'm afraid you have to unpick back to where the mistake was made (use a stitch picker if you have one, or sewing scissors if you don't). Get mad, calm down, learn from your mistake.

Something doesn't look right, but I can't work out what. Are all your stitches facing the same way? They should be. Always make sure the first diagonal stitch of every cross stitch is made in the same direction.

The masterclass

JAMIE 'MR X STITCH' CHALMERS

ON TURNING A PICTURE INTO A CROSS-STITCH PATTERN
THE UK'S MOST PROLIFIC MALE EMBROIDERER (OR
'MANBROIDERER', IF YOU WILL) IS THE GO-TO GUY FOR ALL THINGS
CONTEMPORARY, QUIRKY AND INTRIGUING IN THE WORLD OF
NEEDLECRAFT. *mrxstitch.com*

LEARN THE BASICS

A cross-stitch design is basically just a pixelated image, and any image can be reduced to pixels (very small squares of colour). Simple shapes are much easier to turn into a pixelated image, but a photo could be done if you have enough time and patience (although you could pay a professional to do this for you online, or buy a cross-stitch pattern programme for your computer). Because cross stitch is like painting with numbers, you must create a key: symbols that correspond to the colour threads you will use.

GATHER YOUR MATERIALS

Buy tracing paper with graph lines and a sharp pencil. Beginners should stick to a small palette of colours, so you may have to simplify your image; if your source design has a lot of shades and tones of the same colour, use a single colour of thread for all of these (think Warhol-esque).

CREATE THE PATTERN

Lay the tracing paper on top of the image: for each square that has a particular colour behind it, add the relevant symbol (red might be a dot, blue a cross, and so on – or use coloured pens instead of symbols). When the image is complete, you're ready to stitch.

CHANGING THE SCALE

If your source image is larger or smaller than you want your final cross stitch to be, don't use tracing graph paper. Instead, draw a grid directly on to your source image, then transfer the colour details to a separate piece of graph paper.

OR, DO IT FROM SCRATCH

Using coloured pencils and graph paper, design your own cross-stitch paper freehand, without tracing a source image. Start simple, with letters, words or basic shapes.

INSIDER TRICKS

'Keep your thread no longer than the distance between your wrist and elbow. This stops it becoming worn and allows you to get into a rhythm with your stitching rather than having to pull through a long thread after each stitch.'

JESSICA ALDRED, CO-AUTHOR OF *ADVENTURES IN NEEDLEWORK*

jessicaaldred.co.uk

'Mix and match your materials. I have added mini pom-poms to designs, or used knitting wool instead of embroidery thread.'

JACQUI PEARCE, NEEDLEPOINT DESIGNER

grannyknits.co.uk

The project

THE CROSS-STITCH BAG

Put your stitching to good use, rather than filling your bottom drawers with unwanted embroideries. (Because there are only so many cross-stitch pictures one house can take.)

HOW HARD IS IT TO DO?
It's not. At all.

HOW LONG DOES IT TAKE?
Think of it as a chance to watch a few of your favourite movies.

MATERIALS

1. Hessian bag
2. Embroidery thread
3. Needle
4. Alphabet chart
5. Fabric
6. Scissors
7. Tailor's chalk
8. Ruler
9. All-purpose thread

STEP 1
What do you want written on the side of your bag? You can have whatever you want, because I've produced a handy alphabet chart for you to follow (find it on page 218–20). The only limit you have is the size of your bag. Check your chosen phrase will fit before you start stitching, and plan colours, too: will each letter or word be a different colour? Or will you stick to two colours?

STEP 2
Rather than stitching an 'X' over a single square, you'll be stitching it over four. It means you can finish this project in a quarter of the time it would usually take.

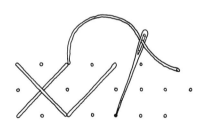

STEP 3

Now to stitch! The easiest way to do this on a hessian bag is to turn it upside down (I poke the needle in with my right hand, then with my left hand inside the bag, use this to guide the needle through and poke it back up). Turn the chart upside down, too and it'll be far easier to follow. Start with the words on the bottom line (in this case, 'Mulberry'), then work up to the top.

STEP 4

Once you've stitched, you can make a lining for your bag: this hides the back of your stitching (which might be messy), and stops the contents of your bag ripping the stitches and unravelling your hard work. You need to cut five pieces of fabric. The first two pieces are as tall as the height of the bag and as long as the width (plus 1cm/^{1}/$_2$in seams all the way around). The second two are the height and the depth of the bag (plus 1cm/^{1}/$_2$in seams). The last is the width and the depth of the bag.

STEP 5

Pin the pieces together so they form a bag-like shape, as in illustration. Backstitch the four long sides first, 1cm (^{1}/$_2$in) away from the edge of the fabric, then stitch the bottom piece on. The seams will be on the outside, but when you look inside it, it looks all neat, right?

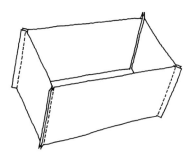

STEP 6

At the moment the top edge of your lining is the rough edge of the fabric. To remedy that, fold it over 1cm (^{1}/$_2$in) all the way around (so the rough edge sits on the outside of the insert), and pin it in place.

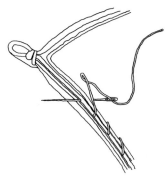

STEP 7

Put the lining inside the bag, so the top edges line up (the corners of your lining should sit nicely in the corners of the bag). Oversew it to the bag (see page 18) in a thread of a complementary colour, removing the pins as you go.

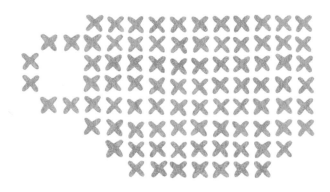

The extras

GO LARGE

Rules were made to be broken, so just because I've told you a cross stitch should be sewn across four holes in a piece of aida, it doesn't mean you have to listen (I didn't in the previous project). What about making giant cross stitches that are two, four or eight aida squares wide? Sure, the pattern you use will need to be as simple as possible (think symbols, silhouettes and letters), but it's a new take on a very traditional craft.

THROW AWAY THE THREAD

Some of my favourite cross stitch isn't actually stitched, but is painted/printed/drawn on to the front of birthday cards, notepads, T-shirts, or even walls (this makes an awesome giant mural). Use a soft pencil and ruler to divide your surface into a grid, then work from the cross-stitch pattern, adding the right-coloured 'X' into each square where relevant (or work by eye). Once dry, rub out the pencil marks and you're left with a beautiful, unexpected, less crafty version of cross stitch.

A WALL OF ART

You could hang a single piece of cross stitch in a bog-standard frame, but you'd make a bigger impact if you framed it within an embroidery hoop (just pull the extra fabric sprouting out at the sides towards the back and tack it in place) and grouped a collection of different cross-stitched pieces together. Unify images by colour or size or shape, or have some kind of theme (birds/teacups/punctuation/musical instruments. The less traditional, the better).

USE IT UNEXPECTEDLY

Swap a ribbon around a trilby for a strip of cross stitch; add a tiny piece of cross stitch to a locket instead of a photo; make a clutch from a piece of cross stitch rather than a piece of fabric … Be creative with the way you use cross stitch and it becomes a much more interesting craft. So long as you don't snip through the stitches and unravel the whole picture, anything goes.

It's knitting, but not as you know it

The woolly phenomenon of guerrilla knitting has delighted and bemused the world in equal measures over the best part of the last decade. But what exactly is the point of a knitted lamp-post cosy? Here, three very different knitters explain the method behind the sneaky stitching madness …

'I WANT TO LEAVE A LITTLE MARK ON THE WORLD'

Known to most as **Lauren O'Farrell**, the founder of the UK's biggest knitting group, Stitch London, it's her alter ego, Deadly Knitshade, who covers the capital with little knitted marvels *(knitthecity.com)*.

'There's a storytelling aspect to what I do. I never just put knitting up on stuff; it's carefully planned and meticulously designed to make people notice parts of the city they might never have seen otherwise. The sheep on London Bridge weren't put there randomly – they highlighted the peculiar, ancient law that still permits Freeman of London to drive a herd of sheep across it.

'It's also about making a bit of the world my own. Banksy has rightly said that if you own land or business, you can do whatever you want with the world: put ads up, posters up, but for the rest of us it's illegal to make our mark. Knitting is the perfect way to do this. It's unthreatening, it's removable and it doesn't damage anything. So it's not a selfish way to do it: it makes my day, and it can make someone else's, too. What we do can make people laugh, smile and think differently.

'The pieces I spend hours knitting get taken almost straight away; people can never understand why that doesn't upset me. But it's because the knitting on the street is just a tiny part of it: the internet makes it immortal. So anyone visiting my website gets to see my stitching, even if it only lasted a few hours in real life.'

'IT'S ABOUT DOING SOMETHING BADASS WITH KNITTING.'

It would be no overstatement to call **Magda Sayeg** the mother of the new guerrilla-knitting movement. Her crew, Knitta Please, might not have been the first to decorate public places with yarn, but they certainly made the biggest impact *(magdasayeg.com)*.

'Almost ten years ago I brightened up my door handle with a little piece of knitting. We covered a few lamp posts and street signs to brighten up the city and, almost a decade on, this thing has become a phenomenon.'

'It changed the course of my life. I was able to quit my job and now I'm a full-time artist. Ninety-five per cent of what I do now is completely different to what we did in those first few years: I make things for galleries, I lecture, I help create commercials for big-name brands. I'm expanding the boundaries of knitting further than I ever could have imagined.

'But all this is not yarn-bombing. There's obviously relevance, but it's different somehow. The true essence of the yarn-bombing movement is still renegade, it's still subversive, it's done without permission. It's about taking knitting out of that context of being something functional or domestic and doing something badass with it.

'So although I love all the extra stuff, I think it's important that I'm still tied to my roots. And I am. I still cover bits of cities when I'm not getting commissioned, just because I want to. Whenever I'm outside my eyes wander: there should be a knitted strip covering that post, I think. It must be how I naturally respond to the street.'

'WE WANTED TO SURPRISE PEOPLE'

Dutch artists **Jan ter Heide** and **Evelien Verkerk**, aka Knitted Landscape, are unlike most guerrilla knitters as they don't use an urban backdrop for their work; it's the natural world that gets them going *(knittedlandscape.com)*.

'I remember the first time I placed a stone with an orange knitted cover in a rough Irish landscape,' says Jan. 'The effect was mind-blowing for me. I had been used to creating things for galleries, but this was almost like creating an exhibition outside.

'Evelien and I have worked together on other art projects – we like to use textiles – and with Knitted Landscape we wanted to surprise people with a sudden flash of unexpected colour, and make them smile. But it was never random – we covered stones, added mushrooms in a way that had something to do with the surroundings. Everything we did was to try and make the landscape more beautiful.

'While it was very exciting to plant knitted things in the natural world, the pictures we took were actually more important than the act. We had them printed and held an exhibition so people could appreciate how much you can change a landscape with even the smallest thing.

'We don't do it anymore. Partly it's because we don't have the time, but also because the new yarn-bombing movement has nothing behind it. It's fun, but there's no meaning: it's just placing something around a pole for no reason. And everything we did was for a reason.'

LESSONS FROM THE FRONT LINE

I must confess, I'm a guerrilla knitter. Or a yarn-bomber, or yarn-stormer, or a graffiti knitter – whatever you want to call it. Lady Loop is my alter ego, Knit the City my crew, and here are my rules…

- ✂ *Be prepared.* Scout out your location ahead of installing and take measurements.

- ✂ *Be inventive with tools.* How are you going to get that knitting to the top of that building? We've used stepladders, retractable poles and coat hangers.

- ✂ *Carry cable ties.* It's the easiest way to fix knitting to public places.

- ✂ *Expect to be bothered.* If you're doing something out of the ordinary – and sticking knitting up in public places is pretty odd – people are going to ask what you're up to. Take the opportunity to have a nice chat.

- ✂ *Call it a craft, not an art, project.* Especially if the police ask you. It got us out of a tricky situation in Parliament Square once. That's got something to do with 'art' being a bit too political, right?

- ✂ *Accept it'll be nicked.* If you've made something that looks pretty, people will want it for themselves. Take it as a compliment.

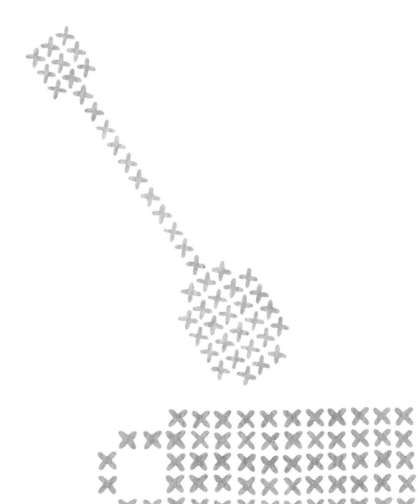

'USE IT UNEXPECTEDLY'

Quilling

Cast away any preconceptions you have about this old-fashioned technique. With the right materials and advice, a few strips of paper can be turned into something incredible.

The technique

MATERIALS

1 Quilling paper
Buy it from craft shops in different colours, textures and widths, from 2mm to 10mm wide.

2 Quilling tool
A cocktail stick, thick sewing needle or similar object will do the job. Or, invest in a specialist quilling tool (yes, there are such things), available in different sizes to create different-sized coils.

3 Glue
Use clear-drying PVA.

4 Paper or card:

5 Tweezers
Oh-so-useful for picking up quills without squashing them.

6 Paper scissors

GETTING STARTED

Traditionally, you would make a series of different shapes – 'quills' – and put them together in such a way that it creates a picture or pattern. This can either look great, or horrendously old-fashioned. That's why contemporary quillers often don't use these shapes at all, preferring to freestyle with strips of paper instead.

MAKING A QUILL

Every basic shape starts with a coil. Wrap a piece of quilling paper around a cocktail stick (or fine sewing needle, if you want the inside to be smaller), leave for a few seconds, then remove: you'll be left with a pretty little coil of paper. Dab a tiny dot of glue on the free end of the paper (using the end of another cocktail stick) and stick it down. Keep hold of the coil until the glue is dry. (If you've bought a fancy quilling tool with a slot, insert the end of the paper into the little slot, then wrap it.)

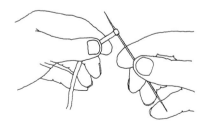

Here's how to make other shapes …

Tight coil: wrap the paper tightly around a sewing needle.

Loose coil: don't leave it wrapped for more than a second, and leave it to uncoil before you glue it.

Teardrop: make a coil, then pinch one end.

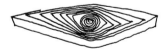

Marquise: make a coil, then pinch both ends.

Square: make a marquise, then pinch the two straight sides.

Triangle: make a teardrop, then pinch the bottom.

Need shapes to be exactly the same size? Then cut several pieces of quilling paper to the same length. Or, if you have some cash to spare, buy a quilling board and drop your coils into the circular-shaped dents.

FREESTYLING

Ditch the cocktail stick; your fingers are the best tools when you want to freestyle. Any shape can be created – really, any shape at all – but here are a few tips for making the basics …

- ✄ *Should you want to make the outline of a shape,* cut the strip a couple of millimetres longer than it needs to be. Bend the shape with your fingers, then overlap the two ends where they join and glue them together here. To make the perfect circle, wrap the strip around something round: a cotton reel or nail-varnish bottle, perhaps.

- ✄ *You could use a cocktail stick* to curl the very end (or both ends) of a long strip, making a swirl. I, however, prefer to use my fingers as it gives me more control.

- ✄ *To make a corner,* fold the strip of paper in half where you want the bend to be, crease, then unfold.

- ✄ *A zigzagged line* can be made by folding the strip up like an accordion.

- ✄ *To create a scalloped line,* pinch at equal points along the length of the paper.

TO FINISH

Dip the tip of a cocktail stick in PVA, and cover the bottom of the shape or the bottom edge of the strip with glue to stick it to your piece of paper. Don't overload it; PVA is surprisingly effective in small amounts. Start with the biggest shapes, or in the centre, and build up your design bit by bit.

COMMON PROBLEMS

My coils don't spring open nicely, or they're too loose. You're either wrapping the paper around the cocktail stick far too tightly, or not tightly enough. Practise, practise, practise and in time you'll learn how much pressure to use.

I can see the glue on my paper base once it's dry. You must be applying too much, or letting it drip on the paper as you put the quill in place.

The masterclass

YULIA BRODSKAYA
ON KEEPING QUILLING CONTEMPORARY

YULIA'S MODERN TWIST HAS SEEN NEW FANS OF QUILLING EMERGE, AND HER WORK GRACE THE FRONT COVERS OF *GUARDIAN* SUPPLEMENTS AND PENGUIN BOOKS, AND APPEAR IN ADVERTS FOR NOKIA, CADBURY AND MANY OTHER COMPANIES. *artyulia.com*

MOVE AWAY FROM THE TRADITIONAL

'I never learned to quill in a traditional manner, perhaps this is why my work became different,' she explains. 'I don't use any basic shapes or special tools and quill-heavy paper or card. I use a cocktail straw and wooden cocktail sticks to roll papers and any sort of paper and card. I use paper in a free way, as if I'm drawing with the paper strips.'

THINK COLOUR

'I try to make my palette as rich as possible,' she says, as this is one feature that sets her work apart from pastel-heavy designs of the more twee hobby quillers.

AVOID CLICHÉD IMAGERY

'Traditional quilling uses mainly florals,' she says. 'I incorporate typography and a lot of objects and motifs that are not obvious for paper.' The fact that she has created people, jukeboxes, ice cream and intricate patterns from strips of paper is another thing that makes her work so unique.

SKETCH EVERYTHING FIRST

'Once I glue a piece of paper I can't remove it, so there is no place for errors. I would advise people to make a very detailed sketch and not start the work until you are absolutely happy with the design'. However, she points out you don't always need to stick to the script: 'There is always room for experiments, because sometimes it is difficult to see what will look good before starting the physical paper work.'

INSIDER TRICKS

ERIN CASNER

ON HOW TO DO QUILLED LETTERING

IN A WORLD FULL OF CRAFT BLOGGERS WHO QUILL, ERIN STANDS HEADS AND SHOULDERS ABOVE THE REST. HER BACKGROUND IN GRAPHIC DESIGN CLEARLY GIVES HER THE EDGE WHEN IT COMES TO CREATING SLEEK AND STYLISH PIECES. *schmancy-ness.blogspot.com*

USE YOUR COMPUTER

'I always start out on a computer, playing with fonts and sizes. Bigger is always best, because it's difficult to be accurate on small letters. Simple, sans serif fonts are easier to work with than serif, ornate ones, too. Print out your letters or words and trace them on to your paper base.

START IN THE RIGHT PLACE

'A right-handed person should start from the left, and vice versa for left-handers, so you don't mess up what's already glued down as you work.

BREAK LETTERS INTO SECTIONS

'Don't try to make letters out of one strip of paper (unless they're very straightforward: an 'O' only needs one strip, or two if you're doing block lettering). It's difficult to glue down a whole letter at a time, so by breaking it up into a few pieces you can be more accurate. Do one section at a time, using a ruler to help you measure and cut strips if you need to. I find that by tearing the ends of the paper rather than cutting them, you can join two strips and it's not terribly noticeable.

MAKE YOUR OWN STRIPS

'If you're struggling to control standard quilling paper, make your own strips from card (a craft knife, metal ruler and cutting mat are all you need). It's harder to get very crisp creases, but it's sturdier, so holds its shape well.

NOW TO PLAY!

'Once the outlines of the letters are done, you're ready to add more details.'

'Serious quillers should invest in a Japanese quilling tool. As the name suggests, it's only available from Japan (and costs about eight times as much as a domestic tool), but it creates amazing super-tiny centres to your coils.'

LEESANDRA DIAZ, FOUNDER OF SWEET SPOT CARD SHOP

sweetspotcards.blogspot.com

'If you want to create large shapes, just glue together multiple strips to get the length of quilling paper you want.'

HONEY MOSER, FOUNDER OF HONEY'S HIVE

honeyshive.etsy.com

The project

A CARD FOR A BIRTHDAY AND BEYOND

Rather than fork out £4 for a card your friend will throw away after the party has ended, make them something they'll want to put in a frame when the hangover has worn off.

HOW HARD IS IT TO DO?

If you're all fingers and thumbs, this one might stretch you.

HOW LONG DOES IT TAKE?

Write off an evening.

MATERIALS

1 **Blank cards/card**

2 **Scissors**

3 **Quilling strips**

4 **PVA glue**

5 **Quilling tool**
   (OR A NEEDLE, COCKTAIL STICK, ETC.)

6 **Pencil/ rubber**

STEP 1

Ready-made blank cards are pretty cheap if you buy them in bulk, or you can make your own by folding a piece of card in half and cutting it to size. (You can buy a natty tool called a 'bone folder' for making the perfect crease. Or make a perfectly acceptable crease with the side of your hand.) I reckon square cards always look more stylish than rectangular ones.

STEP 2

Are you feeling confident? Yes? Then quill directly on to the front of your card. No? No worries; quill on to a piece of paper, then stick this on to the front. Should you make a mistake, you haven't ruined your card base. (Or you can hide the fact you've done this by using the same coloured paper as card and cut it 1mm smaller than the front of the card. Or, make a feature of it: go with a contrasting colour and make it smaller.)

STEP 3

Your first creative job is to decide on the style, size and position of your letter. Anything bold and simple is easiest, anything more detailed will be trickier (but not impossible). Draw it on to a new piece of paper which is either the same colour as your base, or a contrasting one (or trace it from a printout). Cut it out and stick it on the front.

STEP 4

The tutorial on the previous page will show you how to quill the sides of the letters; use the edge of the paper letter as your guide. Take your time and you will get it right.

STEP 5

Now, to decorate. I've gone for simple, long stripes with coils on the end. It's simple, but it works. You might want something more complicated, so try whatever you have time for. When you're done, leave the card to dry.

STEP 6

If you quilled on to a separate piece of paper, now's the time to add it to the front of your card. Using spray mount or double-sided tape is far superior to a glue stick, as neither leave lumps that need to be smoothed out (which is nigh on impossible to do here).

STEP 7

Add a 'Handmade by …' note on the back. If you're feeling particularly precious about sending your masterpiece through the post, send it in a padded envelope, or wrap it in a few sheets of tissue paper. And I reckon a little 'handle with care' note written in thick black marker wouldn't go amiss, either.

The extras

GIVE THE COMPLETE BIRTHDAY PACKAGE

So, you're the kind of person who likes everything – and you mean everything – to match. Once you've made the quilled card from the previous page, consider taking that theme through to the gift, too. Use the same-coloured strips and shapes to decorate a plain tag, and – if you can bear watching your friend rip apart your hard work – the top or sides of the wrapped present as well. I reckon this looks best with crisp white tags and classic brown packing paper.

MAKE QUILLED CARDS, IN BULK

No, I don't mean meticulously creating 20 versions of the same quilled card: none of us have the time (or patience) for that. Instead, quill the most intricate, painstaking one-off, then photograph it in a room filled with natural light. Print it off 20 times and use those copies to decorate the front of your cards. You can still add a 'handmade by …' note on the back. (I'm afraid it's the only way you can do all your Christmas cards or party invites without having to start quilling six months before.)

CREATE A PIECE OF JEWELLERY THAT WILL GET PEOPLE TALKING

I know, paper isn't exactly waterproof or particularly hard-wearing, but use a long-enough strip and you can create some pretty sturdy shapes. Use a tiny dot of superglue to stick quills together, building up a larger, more intricate piece that can be used as a pendant or earring. Secure this to a necklace or earring hook using a jump ring, slipped through the most sturdy part of the shape (see page 180 for more info). Then finish with a coat of varnish; the spray-on stuff will cover the piece most effectively.

PUT IT IN A FRAME

There is no doubt that a beautifully quilled picture deserves a frame; alas, the 3D nature of the craft means it's not as simple as chucking a photo behind a piece of glass. Standard frames can be used – you'll just have to leave the glass out (but be warned: it gets dusty, and because the picture is made from paper, it's a bit of an issue to clean). Or, invest in a posh box frame, which leaves plenty of room for even the deepest quilling. But what should the artist quill? Lettering, of course, looks brilliant, but equally wonderful are random patterns (I like to copy fabric designs that I love), images from magazines or doodles (trace the outline and fill the inside with the quills of different shapes and colours).

TURN EVERYDAY OBJECTS INTO SHOW-STOPPING PIECES

So long as the surface is relatively flat, it can be covered in quills: my general rule is: if you can découpage it, then you can probably quill it, too. Picture frames, boxes, lamp bases, vases and more all look incredible when entirely covered with simple quill shapes (just be sure the item is clean before you stick the quilled paper on to it, and that you use a glue that properly sticks paper to the surface you have). I think glass jam jars look particularly pretty decorated with simple white shapes, with a candle dropped inside.

MAKE AN ORNAMENT FIT FOR A KING

Just as a quilled necklace pendant can be made by sticking several shapes together, a quilled decoration can be made in the same way. Snowflakes are an obvious choice – slip a ribbon through a sturdy quill at the top to hang off your Christmas tree. Or, make a handful of the same shape and thread them on to a long piece of ribbon for an alternative to bunting (extra-large quilled hearts made from thick strips of red cardboard look lovely).

Stitch and bitch

Crafting is far more enjoyable when done with others than on your own. Whether you fancy dipping your toe into the burgeoning craft scene or want to ramp up your local area by hosting your very own group, the founders of some of the UK's best craft groups offer us their pearls of wisdom.

WHAT YOU NEED TO KNOW ... IF YOU'RE GOING TO A GROUP

Your perfect match is out there

Are you after a one-off night of drunken dressmaking, or a regular meet-up with like-minded crafters? Either way, there's sure to be a group for you. 'You'll find everything from tea drinking and zen-like crafting sessions to energetic, noisy, cocktail-drinking craft nights,' explains **Debbie Daniel**, founder of the East London Craft Guerrilla *(craftguerrilla.com)*. Hit the web to work out what's on nearby, but 'The best way to find a group that's suited to you is to go and try it out,' she advises. Of course, if you hate it, you need never go back.

Crucially, look for how the night will play out. Some groups name a venue and you drop in with your own project (usually for free), while others are run like a structured workshop (where you pay to join in).

You have nothing to worry about

It's not a problem if you're entirely useless at making, says **Louise Williams** of Crafty Pint *(handmadeintooting.wordpress.com)*. 'People can come with no prior experience and go away having completed something.'

Just as it's OK to turn up with no crafting skills, so too is it perfectly normal to arrive on your own. 'You won't be alone for too long unless you want to be,' says Debbie. 'Everyone is there because they share a passion for making and they are all very friendly.' Should Debbie's words not reassure you, however, **Francine Schokker** from Birmingham's Creative Open Workshops *(creativeopenworkshops.com)* recommends starting at workshop-based group ('Someone will be in charge so there is less pressure to fit in') or coming to your first event with a friend ('It makes it less daunting').

It's worth knowing the unwritten rules

Do RSVP if you're asked to. 'I have to work out the amount of materials we need and make sure there's enough space,' explains **Nico Dawson**, founder of Manchester craft night Lo-Fi *(manchestercraftmafia.co.uk)*. Check that it's acceptable to bring your own project along ('We run nights on a shoestring budget, so to keep events going we need to make some money through the sales of our craft packs,' Debbie explains). And if everyone is working on their own thing, ask before you copy someone else's design, advises Francine. 'People don't always realise that some of those who come to our drop-in sessions make for a living.'

Buy a drink if you're meeting in a pub or bar (the organiser will have negotiated the space based on the assumption the takings will rise) and remember that the organiser is almost always doing it for love, not money. Be super-polite if you have any complaints, always offer to help clear up, and never, ever ask for an IOU on your fees.

Know what you're letting yourself in for

'It pretty much takes up every single waking moment of my life,' admits Debbie. 'It's non-stop, relentless and a tremendous task.' Consider how much time you can commit to your new group before drawing up too many grand plans. She also advises you to get others on board; you needn't recruit an official committee, but have a few people you can rely on if you're ill/stressed/unmotivated.

The logistics

'The venue is very important,' says Crafty Pint's Louise. Think quiet (so people can chat or you can give demonstrations), well-lit (so people can see to craft) and accommodating (so you don't have a fight on your hands each week/month). Ask pubs, bars, cafés or community halls if you can borrow space in return for extra custom. Or, when the sun is out, meet near an obvious point in a park.

'It needs to be something that is regular,' says Nico, who holds sessions on the first Tuesday of every month. That, or you need to send out a group email with plenty of notice of future dates. Pick an evening that isn't busy – usually at the beginning of the week – and both venues and attendees will be more likely to be free, she suggests.

Whether you charge a fee is up to you, but as Louise says, 'You've got to cover your own costs but also make sure people aren't scared off by the price tag.' (If you need to provide kits, ask people to RSVP their attendance and have a cap on the numbers.) Alternatively, ask people to bring along their own materials and keep the session free.

The creative bit

Venue? Done. Date? Sorted. Now what the hell is everyone going to do when they arrive? 'I wouldn't worry too much on finding a never-been-done-before angle. Just do what suits you and what you can commit to,' says Debbie. The hands-off (and easier) approach is simply letting everyone chat and work on their own project; the hands-on method involves you creating mini workshops each time. Should you fancy that, 'Do a bit of groundwork first and find out what you think people might be interested in,' says Louise. Think about who will teach, too. 'We do a different craft each month, and it's either someone from the Manchester Craft Mafia [the group Nico also runs] or from Lo-Fi who wants to share a skill,' says Nico. Ask local craft shops or makers to help, in return for publicity at the event.

Once the regular stuff is running smoothly, you might want to add a few extras, such as competitions, fairs, or Christmas parties, for example.

Getting people there

'You can never advertise enough,' says Louise. 'We shamelessly publicise in any free listings and use Facebook and Twitter all the time.' Include details of what the night involves and if people should bring anything. Build ties with bigger organisations, she says, such as Etsy and craft magazines. Nico agrees: 'If you can link into any other bigger groups, it helps you to get established.' That might be local craft associations or craft shops, or even pubs or clothes shops. And if there's already a craft group in your area, don't think of them as your rivals, says Debbie. 'Let them know what you're doing. It's not just polite, but could actually be the beginning of something beautiful.'

'NOW
TO PLAY!'

Millinery

The fine art of hat making is now something that anyone can try their hand at. With pre-made bases available relatively cheaply (so there's no need for large studios and clunky hat-blocking equipment), anyone with a basic understanding of the techniques can create something that looks extraordinary.

The technique

MATERIALS

1 Fabric

Sinamay is a mesh-like hat material that many modern fascinators are made from. It can be bought by the metre and – here's a fact for you – it's made from bananas. Felt, straw and other fabrics can be used too, as can any material that has been thickened with stiffener.

2 A fastener

A comb, hair band or piece of elastic.

3 Embellishments

Feathers, beads, sequins and netting is common, but if you can find a way to attach it, anything goes.

4 Needle

It must be sharp (to piece through thick materials) and thicker than usual (so it doesn't break). No sewing machines here, I'm afraid.

5 Thimble

To help you sew through tough sinamay.

6 Multi-purpose polyester or cotton thread

7 Scissors

Use paper scissors for sinamay, as it will blunt fabric ones.

8 Pins

9 Hat base

10 Wire

11 Iron

GETTING STARTED

Work out what you want from your hat. Does it need to make a statement, complement a dress or be suitable for everyday? How you will wear it will affect the fabrics, shapes and size you choose. Look at hats you love for inspiration, and pick out elements that you want to replicate.

THE BASE

From Jackie O pillboxes to Ascot-style discs, almost anything can be found ready-made (and if you can't find the shape you want in a millinery store, buy a hat in the shape you want and replace the decorations). Mini circular bases (think 10–20cm/4–8in in diameter) are typical fascinator fare and cost just a few pounds. Before you buy a base, try it on in front of a mirror and check the shape fits your face.

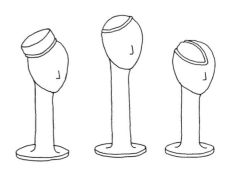

THE DECORATIONS

Some say you can use a hot glue gun to stick embellishments on to a base. And you can. But don't. Great milliners sew everything on by hand, and when you copy what the pros do, your hat is more likely to look as if it were made by a pro.

Stitches should be tiny – no more than 2mm – and as neat as possible. Match the thread to the decoration rather than the base, as it's less noticeable. (Though do remember you can cover up stitching by adding a row of beads or sequins, or masking it with a well-placed feather.)

Whatever embellishments you add from the following list, keep these rules in mind:

✂ *Stick to the 'odd' rule.*
Add three or five feathers, not four or six. Odd numbers of embellishments always look better.

✂ *Consider scale.*
Mix larger embellishments with smaller ones.

✂ *Think about weight.*
Before sewing, pin or tack everything on as best you can, then try the hat on and check it's not too heavy. If it is, it might keep sliding off your head.

READY-MADE EMBELLISHMENTS

Buy fabric flowers, bows, plastic toys, or whatever you find and love. Arrange them nicely, then sew them on. Simple.

SINAMAY

A million different hats can be made with a single strip of sinamay (make it über thin or nice and fat and you'll get very different looks). Buy ready-made (called sinamay bias binding) or craft it yourself. Cut a strip on the bias (page 22) four times wider than it needs to be; fold both edges into the middle, spray with water and iron to hold. Then fold this piece in half and iron again.

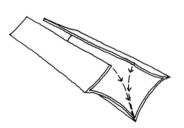

Bend it into shapes while it's still hot – loop it, knot it, make it into a massive bow. Experiment until you love it.

Pin or tack it in place and check yourself out in the mirror before you sew. Snip the ends of the strip on a slant, rather than straight across – it looks far more polished.

Alternatively, cut shapes from sinamay – leaves, petals, bows, etc. – and use your thumbs to roll the edges; this keeps the rough edges tidy. Or, fold the edge over, iron in place, then fold over again to get a neat edge – again, iron in place.

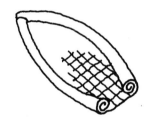

FABRIC AND RIBBON

Sinamay isn't the only material used in millinery: straw and sisal are common, as is felt. But so long as you stiffen it first, almost any fabric or ribbon can be used to decorate. Cut shapes, sew yourself an embellishment (see page 116), then stiffen it to give it structure and longevity. Buy a fabric-stiffening product (available for under a fiver in craft stores) and follow the instructions on the packet (usually you soak the material in the liquid product, then leave it to dry before cutting and shaping).

FEATHERS

Some are fake, some not; some bend easily, some don't; some are massive, some are tiny. Whichever you use, ensure you strip off those little fluffy bits at the bottom. To sew on, hold it in place, and sew over it tightly, as below.

✄ *Curl it.*

Hold the end of the feather in one hand and a pair of scissors in the other. Run the edge of the scissors (not the blade) firmly up the spine, from the bottom to the tip, repeating a couple of times until you get the perfect curl. This works best with pheasant or ostrich plumes.

✄ *Strip it.*

For a strong look, cut one entire side off the feather, then curl as above. Or, to make those little arrow-head feathers that are sold in millinery shops for a fortune, strip both sides of a cockerel or turkey feather, leaving just a couple of centimetres at the top: snip into a diamond or any other shape.

✄ *Bunch them.*

Take a handful of feathers and wrap thread around the stalks, binding them together. Pierce through the middle of the bundle with a needle, then sew them on to the hat base with the same thread.

NETTING

To make a cheeky little veil, cut a large rectangle of netting and do a simple running stitch along three of the edges (leave one long edge free). Use the running stitch as a drawstring, and gather up the netting, using a few stitches to hold it together. Position this on your hat and sew it on when you're happy with how it looks. It is better to add more netting and trim it, than to add too little and have to unpick it (a slanted edge across the face looks lovely). Netting needn't just come across the face; make a bow from it, use it to build height at the back of a hat, or scrunch it up into a ball and put a few stitches through the middle for a flower-like embellishment.

MILLINERY WIRE

This is a simple way to add structural elements to your hat. Bend it into any shape (think petals, leaves and so on) and twist the ends together to secure. Cut a piece of stretchy fabric (cheap coloured tights work really well), and wrap it over the shape, gathering the excess near the twisted ends. Wrap a piece of ribbon around the end (keep it in place with a few stitches) and sew the decoration into place as you would a feather.

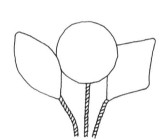

KEEPING YOUR HAT ON

There are a multitude of ways to keep your hat perched on top of your head.

✄ *Elastic:* Buy hat elastic (it's pre-cut and has mini metal rods on either end) and slip the metal ends through the weave of a sinamay base. Or, take a piece of normal elastic, tie a knot in either end, and sew it on either side, as right.

✄ *Comb:* Whether it's plastic or metal, sew it to the underside of your hat, stitching in between each tooth.

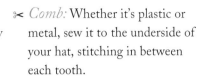

✄ *Hairband or clip:* Hold it flat to the underside and stitch on.

COMMON PROBLEMS

My messy stitching is ruining my hat. You haven't mastered the art of layering yet. Sew the biggest elements on first, then cover the stitching with the smaller embellishments: for example, in this order, add: netting, sinamay strips, feathers.

My sinamay won't bend properly. Are you sure you've cut it on the bias? Go and read page 22 again and check you have.

The masterclass

PHILIP TREACY

ON MAKING A MAGNIFICENT HAT
THE LEGENDARY HAT DESIGNER HAS CREATED SOME OF
THE WORLD'S FINEST HEADPIECES, FOR THE LIKES OF
CHANEL, GIVENCHY AND RALPH LAUREN. HE WAS THE
MOST IN-DEMAND MILLINER AT THE ROYAL WEDDING.
philiptreacy.co.uk

DON'T COPY HIGH-STREET HATS
'I'm certainly not a fan of high-street fascinators,' Philip
says. 'Cheap imitations are leading to the downfall of the
headgear trend that milliners worked so hard to create;
now they are just limp feathers and a tacky flower.'

EMBRACE FEATHERS
'I like to work with all kinds of materials, but birds in
particular are exquisite perfection,' he believes. 'Their
feathers are weightless, they give movement and volume –
they are very sexy. You are drawing with them rather than
just decorating a hat.'

EXPERIMENT WITH CONFIDENCE
'Don't be afraid of being different. Rules are made to
be broken and it is individuality and uniqueness that
will get you noticed,' he says. 'Milliners at the beginning
of their careers can often play it safe.' But, he adds, is
safe really a bad thing? 'You want to create something
that in a hundred years' time people will make people say,
"Wow, who did that?"'

TRY IT ON
Sure, there might be guidelines to hat design, he says, but
'never rules'. 'You will know through your own judgment
when a hat is right. The most important thing is that the
wearer feels happy and confident.' But how do you know
if you've really nailed it? 'Do they smile when they see
themselves in the mirror? Do you see a sparkle in their
eye? That's when you know you've done it right.'

INSIDER TRICKS

'Milliners tend to use a single thread when sewing; this
is because it is a lot less likely to tangle. Also, polyester
thread tangles less than cotton.'

KATE UNDERDOWN, MILLINER

kateunderdown.com

KATHERINE ELIZABETH

ON CREATING A HAT TO BE WORN EVERY DAY

THE ROLL-CALL OF KATHERINE'S FANS IS A LONG AND DISTINGUISHED LINE; SHE HAS WORKED WITH STEPHEN JONES, HELPING TO CREATE HEADPIECES FOR DIOR AND JOHN GALLIANO SHOWS, AND HER HATS HAVE GRACED THE HEADS OF LILY ALLEN, DITA VON TEESE, HENRY HOLLAND AND MANY MORE. *katherineelizabethhats.com*

TONE IT DOWN

'A lot of people are very scared of wearing hats, especially during the day, so we start them off with small headband.' Anything in dark, muted colours often feels more wearable, too, she says, but she also suggests that you choose your hat colour to suit your eyes and skin tone.

GET THE FABRIC RIGHT

'Sinamay is really associated with weddings and occasion wear, so instead I use a lot of felt and leather,' she says. Buy millinery felt, which is thicker and pre-stiffened, and you can create your own bases. Faux fur, too, is becoming increasingly acceptable during the day, she believes.

DON'T GO GIRLY

'You don't want anything too fluffy or feather boa-y. If you're wearing it with a suit or office wear, keep it more architectural.' Feathers are acceptable, she says, but stick to one or three. Sparkles are OK too, she adds, but 'Keep it to the size of a penny.' Or, just add one nice button or bead or some metal studs. (Of course, the 'no girly' rules change a little when it comes to accessorizing a summer dress, in which case, she says, 'You could attach a flower or make a big bow out of fabric.')

MAKE IT VERSATILE

'People think that hats are only for one occasion, but if you pin things on rather than sewing them they can take you from day to night,' she explains. For example, you wouldn't want netting on your daytime hat, but pin a little piece on before you go out for the evening and it can entirely transform it. 'You want a small piece of netting that comes down to a point, rather than something too full,' she advises.

'For me, less is more. Often hats have too much chucked at them. Keep it simple, with one point of focus that works well with the face and head. It's about proportion and balance.'

PIERS ATKINSON, COUTURE MILLINER

piersatkinson.com

The project

THE TAKE-ME-ANYWHERE FASCINATOR

The beauty of this project is that you can make your bow as small (and classy) or as oversized (and statement-y) as you like (or as the occasion demands).

HOW HARD IS IT TO DO?
It's only folding and stitching.

HOW LONG DOES IT TAKE?
Pour yourself a glass of wine and retreat to your craft table for a couple of hours.

MATERIALS

1. Newspaper

2. Sinamay

3. Iron

4. Complementary coloured thread

5. Needle

6. Scissors

7. A hat base

8. A fastener (ELASTIC/COMB, ETC.)

STEP 1
To start, cut two rectangles of sinamay, one larger than the other. Their size depends on how big you want your final hat to be; to make a statement bow, I used a piece that was 60cm by 18cm and another that was 50cm by 16cm. If you're not sure what size will suit you best, follow steps 1–4 using newspaper first, then when you are happy with the size, make it in sinamay.

STEP 2
To neaten the edges of your sinamay rectangles, fold each edge over 1cm (¹/₂in), then one 1cm (¹/₂in) again, and iron in place.

STEP 3
Now turn each rectangle into a bow. To do this, fold both short edges into the middle, so they overlap slightly, then hold these in place with a few tacking stitches using a thread that is the same colour. You can already see the bow taking shape, right? Now do the same for the second rectangle.

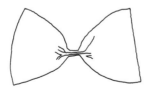

STEP 4
To assemble your hat, lay the smaller rectangle on top of the larger one. Gather both pieces of sinamay in the middle to turn the pieces into bows. This might take a few attempts to get it right, so fiddle with it until you're happy. Stitch the two pieces together to secure (a bulldog clip or similar can come in handy here, to hold the bow shape in place while you sew).

STEP 5
Wrap a strip of sinamay bias binding (see page 105) around the middle of the bows, to hide the messy stitches and give the bow its finishing touch. Stitch it in place. (A nice detail is to make a second, thinner piece of sinamay bias and wrap that around, too, to give the appearance of layers.)

STEP 6
And to finish, sew the whole thing to the middle of a sinamay hat base and add a fastener. If it's a large bow, I suggest a hairband or piece of elastic rather than a comb, as it helps it stay on your head better.

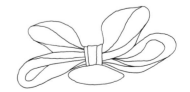

The extras

THE EMERGENCY HAT

It's a disaster! You didn't realise hats were obligatory at tomorrow's wedding/race day/birthday party, and the shops are closed for the evening. Even the craft box is fresh out of hat bases. But don't worry, because in extreme situations like this (or when you're short of cash) cheats are acceptable, and this DIY fascinator base will do just fine for one outing (and maybe more).

Cut a circle from a piece of card and cut a slit into the middle: fold it over 1cm so it becomes a shallow cone and staple it to secure. Now, cut a circle of fabric twice the size of your card circle and sew a running stitch all the way around the edge: rather than securing the thread with a knot, leave the end of it long. Lay the fabric circle down, wrong-side up, and place the cone on top, point facing down. Pull the ends of the thread, like a draw string, so the fabric covers the cone, and oversew the middle closed. Decorate the fabric cone and attach it to a clip as usual.

GIVE AN OLD HAT AN UPGRADE

Whether it's a bowler, a boater or a Trilby, every hat needs a lick of paint every now and again. Vintage hats look especially shiny when you upgrade a part (as do cheap sinamay hats bought from charity shops).

Use sewing scissors or a stitch ripper to remove any old hat bands wrapped around the base, trim loose bits of thread or straw and give the whole hat a good dust down. Should your hat band be stuck down with glue, carefully pull it away. Measure the diameter of the hat where the new band will sit, using a tape measure, then cut a piece of ribbon 2cm ($^3/_4$in) longer (or make a strip of fabric in the same way as you would make a strip of sinamay, on page 105). Fold the ribbon in half and sew together with a line of backstitch 1cm ($^1/_2$in) from the ends, so that it makes a loop. Slip this over the hat and position the join line at the side.

Some say you can glue your new band in place, but I disagree: I'd rather add a few discreet stitches on either side, so it's easier to replace next time. A little bow, made from the same type of ribbon, looks great sewn over the join – you'll find instructions for that on page 116 – or sew flowers, feathers or other embellishments to your new band.

IF YOU DON'T LIKE HATS

Should your newly found millinery skills end up gathering dust, you can put them to better use making brooches instead.

Sandwich a piece of card between two pieces of felt and oversew them together; this becomes your brooch base. Add embellishments in the same way as you would when making a hat (sinamay knots look especially great, because the material holds its structure), but keep it low-key and ensure that it's not too heavy. Stitch a brooch back on to your felt base to finish it off.

Your millinery skills will take you far at a masked ball or Halloween party, too. Get yourself a plain mask base and stitch feathers, embellishments and sparkles on (use a leather needle, as on page 142–143, or a thimble, if you find it tough to pierce the plastic).

Curled feathers look smashing sewn to one side, as an asymmetrical mask always suggests a touch of class. I'll allow you to use a blob or two of glue if you must, but remember – get the wrong type and you'll have bits and bobs falling off before the After Eights are served.

Dudes of craft

Men make too, you know. The history books are full of blokes crafting their own stuff: soldiers, sailors and shepherds have snipped and stitched in past centuries, as have modern icons such as President Franklin Roosevelt and the actors Cary Grant and Russell Crowe (though no one's sure if the last one has done it more than once for a PR stunt). But craft today is seen as a sport for girls, so what do the twenty-first-century men who make think about that?

'MOST PEOPLE ASSUME I HAVE A CREW OF SEAMSTRESSES'

The textile artist **Ben Venom** blends two very different cultures – patchworking and heavy metal – and in doing so creates some very unusual and impressive quilts. *(benvenom.com)*

'My friends thought it was pretty ridiculous when I first started making quilts, but they soon got that I was serious about my work. That said, I still get jokes when I'm at the bar and a friend introduces me: "This is Ben Venom ... he makes quilts." Once I've explained what I do in more detail – that I patchwork with heavy-metal band T-shirts – the awkward looks disappear. Perhaps it's because I collide quilt-making with metal, a very macho musical genre, or because I hang out with a lot of metal heads and artists, so it's easier for them to get what I'm doing.

'Still, most of the time people don't think I'm the one who actually sews: they assume I have a crew of seamstresses making the quilts for me in my basement and all I do is provide the design. That couldn't be further from the truth. It's my hand doing the work from step one to the finish.

'I'm just like any other bloke. I like to watch football, bad action movies and documentaries ... I just like to embroider while I do all that. I'm sure there is a stigma about men who craft, but I couldn't care less. At the end of the day whatever is produced should be able to stand alone, regardless of the gender of the person who created it.'

'I'M MAN ENOUGH FOR ME, EVEN WHEN I'M KNITTING'

Sunday Times journalist **John-Paul Flintoff**, and author of *Sew Your Own*, is partial to a bit of make-do-and-mend, and can often be found patching holes in his wife's shirts and making his own jeans. *(flintoff.org)*

'My sister taught me to knit when I was seven, so I made a jumper for my teddy. But I didn't knit again for years. I learned sewing at school only very reluctantly (it was compulsory), but again, I did nothing with it. Then I married somebody with no practical skills (but charming in every other way) and became the person who sewed on buttons and did the other small, necessary repairs. We had a daughter, and in due course I made outfits for her teddy bears. And then I started making the bears themselves.

'Having achieved a modest level of skill, I decided to take on something incredibly difficult: a fitted shirt. If I say so myself, it was a work of genius. I wore it every day for weeks (but did wash it at night). So I decided to make an entire outfit, right down to the underpants. People usually look horrified when I tell them this, but only for a brief moment. Once they've checked out my clothes, they tend to look impressed.'

'I am conscious that I get more credit than I would if I were a woman doing the same thing: and though that isn't particularly fair for women, it's pretty nice for me. I'm the only man in my family to do this kind of thing, but none of them are against it in any way. If others are, that's their problem. I'm man enough for me, even when I'm knitting.'

'SOME GIRLS THINK MEN AREN'T SUPPOSED TO CRAFT'

Phil Davidson is the founder of Urban Cross Stitch, and the mastermind behind the iconic Banksy kits that helped shake up the dreary world of cross stitch. *(urban-cross-stitch.com).*

'When I sold my cross-stitch kits on a stall on Brick Lane market, I would always sew to pass the time. I think because people saw a guy doing it, they took more notice of my stall and my products. Plenty of men would come up to see what I was doing, and I liked that they weren't put off because it was craft. Weirdly, however, when their girlfriends realised I was doing cross stitch they'd pull them away. I guess because some girls think men aren't supposed to do that sort of thing.

'But I have found that lots of men do. My customers are about 40 per cent guys and 60 per cent women. I'm sure much of that is because I design things that appeal to me – cross-stitch street art, computer games or records – so a lot of other guys can identity more with the images I'm working with, far more than the usual kittens-and-puppy-themed kits out there.

'I didn't know any men who crafted before I started Urban Cross Stitch. Actually, I had never cross-stitched myself before I was 27. It was a grandmother in Arkansas who taught me while I was on a three-month career break, having just given up my job as a pattern cutter in a London couture house. None of my friends were particularly surprised when I came back to the UK and started the business – they are all very creative, either in the fashion world or studied art. It was my mother and my brother who were most surprised, but not because I'm a bloke doing a traditionally female thing, but because they wondered how on earth I was going to make any money from it.'

Embellishments

Because we've all got a plain, battered bag, dress or cushion in the back of a cupboard that could do with a makeover.

The technique

MATERIALS

1 **Fabric**
Absolutely any type goes.

2 **Medium needle**.

3 **Multi-purpose cotton or polyester**

4 **Fabric scissors**

5 **Iron**

GETTING STARTED

How you craft these embellishments depends entirely on your taste. If you're after a chic, minimalist look, make them petite, in neutral tones. On the other hand, if you like to make a statement, do them big, in outlandish colours.

MAKE A BOW

This is the classic fabric embellishment. Cut a long strip of fabric twice as wide and tall as you want your final bow to be. With the fabric right-side down, fold the long top and bottom edges into the middle, run an iron along it to hold the crease, then fold both the short edges into the middle, too. Again, iron them in place. Sew two lines of running stitches down the middle, but don't secure: instead, push the fabric down the thread so it gathers nicely, and use a few stitches to hold it in place.

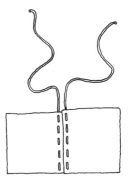

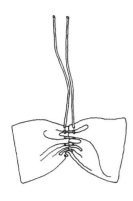

To make the middle, cut a small strip of fabric (about half the width of the first strip you cut, long enough to wrap it around the middle) and fold both long edges into the middle. Iron to hold in place. Wrap it around the centre of the bow and stitch it at the back to secure.

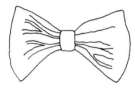

Transforming this into a pussy bow (you know, those bows that look like they have legs) is easy: cut two long, thin strips with slanted ends (as long as you'd like them to be in relation to the bow) and pin them together, right sides facing. Sew around the edge, leaving a small opening in the middle, and use this to turn it the right way around. Iron flat, oversew the opening closed, and stitch to the back of your bow.

MAKE A RUFFLE

Use a thin strip of fabric and these look simple and pretty; use something thick and they'll be luxurious and statement-y. Cut your strip about two-and-a-half times the length you want it to be when finished (or more, if you want über ruffles). If your fabric frays, cut it with pinking shears or hem both long edges. Or, use ribbon as an alternative.

Sew a running stitch along the length of the strip, down the middle or at one edge, but don't secure it at the end with a knot; instead, take the thread in one hand, and use the other to gather up the fabric. Knot the thread so that the ruffle can't unravel, then rethread the needle and sew a few securing stitches to hold.

Your ruffles needn't look so uniform, though. Use a long triangle of fabric rather than a strip or add an extra strip for a double ruffle.

MAKE A FABRIC CLUSTER

These little decorations can be stitched to anything – on their own or in large clusters – to add texture and volume. Cut a circle or square from your fabric and pinch the middle.

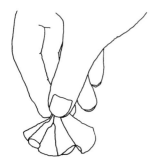

Stitch through the pointed end that you just created a few times, about 1cm away from the top, to hold this ruffled shape in place.

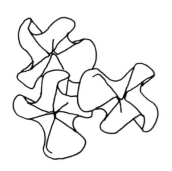

READY-MADE FRINGES, EDGING AND TRIMS

Any haberdashery will be filled with beautiful trimmings with which you can decorate your textiles. Just remember, not all will withstand a washing machine, so don't embellish things you're not happy to hand wash.

✄ *Ribbons can be sewn on by hand or with a machine,* but they do require a fine needle so as not to damage the fibres. Pin them in place on your fabric (never in the centre, always 1mm from the edge where you will eventually sew, so that the stitches cover any holes the pins may leave), and backstitch down each edge.

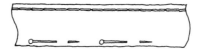

✄ *Lace, and other super-decorative trims,* are best hand sewn. Stitches shouldn't be seen, so keep them as small and as neat as possible, and place them where needed so they don't ruin or disrupt the design.

✄ *Fringing or beaded edging* can be sewn on to the back of the fabric so that only the decorative dangling bits can be seen. (Pin in place, then check from the front that the decorative beads, not the fabric strip, is on show.) Or, sew the fabric strip directly on to the front.

COMMON PROBLEMS

My bow/ruffle/cluster looks too floppy. If you've gone for the super-size option, a bow made from cotton or a similar material is going to flop. To make something more perky, pre-stiffen the fabric with a spray called 'fabric stiffener', available from good craft shops, or add a stabiliser to the back before you stitch it up (see page 18).

'EMBRACE
THE CLASH'

The masterclass

LIBERTY
ON WORKING WITH PATTERNED FABRIC

EMMA MAWSTON IS HEAD OF DESIGN FOR LIBERTY ART FABRICS, THE WORLD'S MOST LUSTED-AFTER RANGE OF HERITAGE AND CONTEMPORARY MATERIALS. *liberty.co.uk*

LOOK AT THE SIZE OF THE PRINT
'It is important to consider the product when deciding on your design. A large scale floral won't look its best on a tiny bow,' she explains.

YOU CAN MIX PATTERNS
'People often think it is necessary to balance pattern with plain, but this doesn't always have to be the case,' Emma says. She has a few simple tricks to help you match pattern with pattern if you're not yet confident in your own taste: choose different fabrics with the same colours running through them. Or, use the same pattern of fabric in different colourways. 'Interesting and unique combinations can be created using an eclectic mix of print or more subtle and harmonious pieces by using fabrics with the same colour hues or one design in varying colour shades.'

REMEMBER WHICH WAY IS UPSIDE DOWN
'Prints are generally created to be used any way up on a product, but sometimes – as in the case of prints in the Art Nouveau style – designs are created in one direction. Although I am all for experimenting with print, I am quite passionate about using directional prints in the way they were intended.' When cutting pieces from your fabric, check that they'll be the right way up when you stitch them together.

OR, USE IT UNCONVENTIONALLY
'It is good to be innovative and unconventional with fabric use: this creates originality and personalises your product,' she says. It's OK if you like the back of the fabric more than the front, or prefer your triangles point-side down. And if you've never considered using prints in anything but the conventional way, experiment with other ways they might work.

FABRIC SHOULD NOT BE A SECOND THOUGHT
'You could spend hours making the most amazing product, but if the fabric you use is neither beautiful nor of sentimental value your time will be wasted time,' she advises. 'As with cooking, the best ingredients always make the best product.' Wise words indeed.

TRUST YOUR GUT
'Everyone has their own instinct about what fabric they like,' Emma believes. 'Go with that. As long as you're happy and really love it, that's all that is important at the end of the day.'

INSIDER TRICKS

DANIELLE PROUD

ON EMBELLISHING YOUR HOME WITH STYLE
THIS INTERIOR DESIGNER KNOWS GOOD CRAFT. NOT ONLY IS SHE A FORMER HEAD DESIGNER AT BIBA WHO HAS STYLED MANY OF LONDON'S TOP CLUBS AND RESIDENCES, SHE HAS ALSO SEWN COUTURE FOR VIVIENNE WESTWOOD AND IS THE AUTHOR OF *HOUSE PROUD: HIP CRAFT FOR THE MODERN HOMEMAKER*. *danielleproud.com*

USE EMBELLISHMENTS AS 'DESIGN GLUE'

'In every room you should have three main anchors – a great mirror or a sofa, for example. Everything else should complement them in some way, acting as design glue. This rule should help you choose the colour, pattern or texture of your embellishments. (Even those mismatched rooms you see in magazines are never randomly thrown together.)

BE PRACTICAL

'Don't get carried away with the look of a project: remember, you have to be able to use whatever you're embellishing. Is delicate silk really the right fabric to decorate a cushion with when you know it goes through a lot of wear and tear?

KEEP IT SIMPLE

'People who come from a craft background can have a tendency to over-embellish. The trick is 'less is more'. Embellish your curtains and a few cushions with a pom pom trim, for example, and your handiwork can really sing. Go for five different trims in the same room, however, and you'll lose that effect.

BE CAREFUL BUYING FABRIC ONLINE

'Make sure you look at colour, pattern *and* texture when you're choosing fabric. Texture is such an important feature of fabric, because it can look so great to layer different textures on top of each other. However, it's an element you can't really assess when you buy pieces from the internet.

HANDMADE DOESN'T HAVE TO MEAN 'SHABBY CHIC'

'I veer away from anything too pretty or that looks shabby chic as I love fabrics with geometric patterns. Something like a stripe will have an impact as soon as you walk into a room, unlike something you have to look at for half an hour to take in all of the elements.'

'Making flowers is a simple way to use up small scraps of ribbon and odd buttons. Stitch loosely up one side of a 10–15cm (4–6in) length of ribbon, pull the thread taught so that the material forms a flower shape and stitch the ends of the ribbon closed. Finish by adding a button to the middle and – voila! – a beautiful flower.'

HANNAH READ-BALDREY, CRAFTER, AUTHOR AND STYLIST

couturecraft.blogspot.com

'Using iron-on fusible webbing you can turn any piece of fabric into an embellishment. Iron it on to the back of a leopard-print fabric, then cut out the individual spots: iron these on to a colourful printed fabric for a psychedelic animal print. Or, cut off the wide patterned edges (*pallu*) from saris, iron fusible webbing on to the back, then use it to decorate your projects.'

MOMTAZ BEGUM-HOSSAIN, CRAFT AUTHOR AND BLOGGER

momtazbh.co.uk

The project

THE NO-ZIP CUSHION COVER

Because no matter how dingy, every rented flat or newly bought house looks brighter when there are a few lovely cushions scattered around the place.

HOW HARD IS IT TO DO?

There's no zip, so even beginners will be OK.

HOW LONG DOES IT TAKE?

Your sofa will be a nicer place to sit in just an hour or two.

MATERIALS

1 Fabric

2 Ruler

3 Tailor's chalk

4 Fabric scissors

5 Pins/iron

6 Needle

7 All-purpose thread

STEP 1

Cut a piece of fabric that is as wide as your cushion and two-and-a-half times as long. (I know what you're thinking – shouldn't there be 1cm seams here? Well spotted. We're deliberately not adding this so the cushion fits snugly inside the cover and looks nice and plump.)

STEP 2

Lay the fabric right side down. On one of the short edges, fold 1cm over, then over again: iron or pin this in place. Sew it neatly using a backstitch. Repeat for the other short end of the fabric.

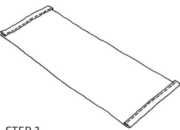

STEP 3

With your fabric still right-side down, place the cushion in the middle. Fold the edges of the fabric up over it – they will overlap. Is your cushion sitting snug inside? Yes? Good news. Use tailor's chalk to mark where the edges of the fabric reach.

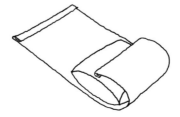

STEP 4

Remove the cushion, because now is the time to make your embellishments. Go for bows, clusters, frills: whatever you fancy. Do them in a contrasting or the same fabric (I reckon this looks classiest). Make just one embellishment, or cover the whole thing and make a statement.

STEP 5

You know where the front of the cushion is, so unfold the fabric from around the cushion, and pin the embellishments on. Wrap the fabric around the cushion again to check the embellishments are positioned in the right place, then sew them on.

STEP 6

Lay the fabric right-side down again and fold the edges to the marks you made in step 3. Pin in place, then stitch down both sides of the cover, 1cm from the edge, using a backstitch, so that there is only a gap left in the back of the cushion cover.

STEP 7

Turn your cushion cover the right way around, then whack the cushion in through the gap in the back. And while you're in a cushion-making mood, why not do a few more? They needn't be identical to look brilliant.

The extras

THE EMBELLISHED ACCESSORIES

Quick – learn how to make a fabric necklace (see page 182) and then you're ready to make a simple piece of statement jewellery. Use up crazy-coloured scraps by stitching fabric clusters to this necklace base (because it's easier to get away with purple metallic Lycra on jewellery than it is on clothing). Glue a coiled-up ruffle on to a ring base for an unusual cocktail ring. Slip a jump ring through the loop of a bow for a cute set of earrings (see page 180). Or perhaps glue ribbon or decorative edging around a plastic bangle. It doesn't stop at jewellery either. Add fringing/lace/beaded strips to the ankle strap of a shoe, the edge of a shawl or scarf, a hair band, the hem of a skirt or much, much more. The list goes on …

THE TAKE-ME-ANYWHERE BROOCH

Sometimes that plain dress or T-shirt or jacket isn't quite special enough. Sure, you could sew a giant bow on the shoulder, or add a line or two of ruffles down the front, but you don't want it to stay there forever; you just need it for tonight. That's when I call in the take-me-anywhere brooch.

Sew your embellishment on to a circle of felt and then stitch a brooch pin to the back of the circle. And voilà! A versatile accessory you can add or remove as and when you wish. Pin a few around one shoulder of a jumper or to the collar of a coat and then, once you're bored with it, take it off and pin it to something new.

GLAM UP YOUR UNMENTIONABLES

Crafted underwear sounds horrific, I know, but bear with me here. Think about any expensive bra and knicker sets you own; they are only pricey because they are covered in lavish embellishments. Adding your own piece of beautiful lace to the top of a bra isn't so bad, is it? And stitching a tiny red bow on the back of a pair of French knickers is hardly the worst thing in the world.

But if you really can't handle that, consider tarting up a bikini instead. Plain, mismatched tops and bottoms can be made to look like a pair if you add the same detail to both: a smattering of bows or the odd ruffle. Failing all of that, if you're the kind of girl who wears ankle socks with her heels, you'll know it looks much prettier when you've got a little ruffle or bow stitched on, too.

SINGLE NO MORE

Most people just think to add one ruffle, one bow or one flower as an embellishment, but I reckon these details look far better in bulk. Cover both shoulders of a T-shirt with fabric clusters; stick bows all over a wooden bangle; stitch ruffles all over one side of a tote bag, or draw an angular shape – a square, triangle or hexagon – on to a cushion, dress or set of curtains, and stitch embellishments, strips of ribbon or lace inside it. The structural, architectural shaping of something like this keeps it looking fresh, not quaint.

If you're still concerned that the piece looks too crafty, make embellishments from the same colour as your base fabric, and play with different tones or textures to create interest instead.

Drop stitches, not bombs

A new generation of activists stitch, not shout, their slogans. But can gentle crafting really do more than a good old placard-filled protest? Betsy Greer, the crafter, activist and author who first coined the term 'craftivism', gave me the inside track …

'You might think it bizarre to mix craft and activism. The latter is soft and safe, the other hard and scary. I thought so, too (I think we're culturally entrenched to see things this way). But after a few years of being part of unfulfilling, traditional activism – marches and chanting and the like – I began to wonder why activism couldn't be as pleasant and appealing as a hand-knitted scarf.

'I was always left so frustrated at the end of a traditional protest. All the yelling seemed to close down the dialogue and shut outsiders out. I would get home torn between feeling like I had made a difference and feeling like I might as well have never left the house. However, I knew that when I had crafted in public, random strangers were very happy to approach me, and ask me about what I was doing. Sometimes people would look at me bemused (perhaps understandably) while with others you could see the wheels in their head turning as they thought more about it. That, I felt, is what real activism should be about: getting people to ask questions, and think about a side of the situation they'd never considered before.'

CRAFTIVISM IN ACTION

'In the years that I have been writing about and taking part in craftivism it has taken many forms, from knitting blankets for the local homeless shelter to embroidering banners to show off thoughts on economic injustice. Or from crafting outfits from scratch so you don't have to buy unethically produced clothes, to yarn-bombing your street with a political theme in mind. 'Craftivism' has come to be used as an umbrella term for all the craft done in the name of making the world a better place.

'And I believe that this approach can be very effective – perhaps even more so than traditional protests. Chanting in large numbers might make your views heard, but the people who aren't involved tend to shy away from the noise. Making work quietly, however, in a medium that people are familiar with (so many of us still equate it with the safety of our mothers and grandmothers), encourages people to come forward of their own accord and ask questions. Why have you chosen to stitch that slogan and hang it on a lamp post, rather than making a pretty picture for your bedroom wall?

'I have found that most of these enquiries go beyond mere curiosity: people seek to truly understand your work and the point it is making, without you needing to raise your voice to be noticed. You'd be hard pushed to find this process blossoming in a traditional activist march.'

CONTINUED OVERLEAF

'But what I and many other modern craftivists are doing is not actually that new. There are incredible tapestries done by women in Chile who use thread to depict the horror of the Pinochet regime in the 1970s, despite the fact they could be killed for speaking against the government. In both the world wars (and other wars, both previous and post these two) women and children have knitted socks, clothes and bandages to show their support for soldiers. In South Africa, women have made wall hangings that show what daily life is really like when you have HIV and/or AIDS. Turning your craft into your mouthpiece has a rich, long history that spans the world.

'I'm frequently asked whether a certain piece of craft is a piece of craftivism, and I generally respond the same way, with the following questions: "Why are you making it?"; "What's the story behind it?" I find that 99 per cent of pieces that can be considered acts of craftivism are made by people who want to change the world in some way, or help others, whether they know these "others" personally or not. Once asked, people generally start to pour out their stories to me, about an issue/illness/cause/wrong that they want to fix/eradicate/raise awareness of. And mostly, I find, they didn't even realise they were being a craftivist.'

TWO CRAFTIVISTS TO BE INSPIRED BY

Sarah Corbett
is the founder of the Craftivist Collective, the London-based group that raise awareness of global poverty and human rights injustice (*craftivist-collective.com*).

'The process of crafting gives people that time to really think about why they are making something – it can be far more engaging than simply signing a petition. In the busy world we live in, I don't think we don't give ourselves enough time to sit still and reflect on the issues that are important to us.'

Carrie Reichardt
aka the Baroness, is a ceramacist best known for her anarchic pottery and glorious mosaics (*carriereichardt.com*).

'Highly skilled craftwork is always a labour of love, and it is this recognition of time and skill that allows the audience to engage in a piece that can challenge their views and beliefs. I also love to upcycle old, vintage, ceramic pieces: apart from the fact you are working with such beautiful artefacts to begin with, they are also so loaded with connotations that it is a joy to be able to subvert their meaning.'

'DROP STITCHES NOT BOMBS'

'USE
TEXTURE
NOT JUST
COLOUR'

Paper cutting

Master some knife-wielding basics and turn any old piece of paper into something worthy of a frame. You can create simple and elegant designs straight away, and in no time at all you'll be producing intricate, beautiful pieces of paper art.

The technique

MATERIALS

1 Paper or card
Acid-free lasts longer, but you can use anything (even pages of magazines or maps or newspaper). Paper is easier to cut but flimsy; card is sturdy but more difficult to slice.

2 Knife
Whether you buy disposable or one with replaceable blades, make sure you feel comfortable holding it.

3 Cutting mat
Invest in an A4-sized self-healing one.

4 Ruler
A metal knife needs a metal blade, so never use a ruler made of plastic. A 30cm (12in) one is perfect for most projects.

5 Small, sharp paper scissors

6 Soft-lead pencil and rubber

7 Tweezers
Not vital, but can help remove tricky bits of paper you've just cut out.

GETTING STARTED

You've got to get comfortable and confident. Wielding a craft knife when you're nervous is a shortcut to a shoddy paper cut and sliced fingers.

Warm up with some cuts on a piece of scrap paper: some prefer to hold their knife like a pen, others place their finger on top, but always keep the knife at 45 degrees to the paper.

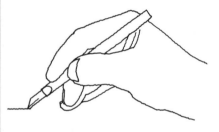

PREPARING THE PATTERN

Very simple patterns can be drawn directly on to the paper, then cut out; leftover pencil lines can then be rubbed out carefully to avoid any ripping. But for anything more detailed (which would inevitably rip if you took a rubber to it), design your pattern on a thin piece of paper first (or print out a ready-made design from the internet/photocopy it from a paper-cutting book). Lay this on top of the paper you want to use, using masking tape to secure the two pieces together.

MAKING THE CUT

Cut out the biggest chunks of the pattern first, then focus on the details. Work from left to right if you're right-handed (vice versa for lefties). Start each cut in a corner of a shape, and try not to stop until you get to another corner, so you get a nice smooth line. Keep it slow but steady and apply even pressure. If your knife feels like it's being dragged over the paper, it probably is – change the blade. Never hold your hand in an awkward position to cut; rotate the paper instead (even while cutting, if it helps).

Only when you have finished cutting the paper should you push out any areas that are to be removed. Ignore the temptation to pull away a chunk of paper that doesn't lift out easily, rather, go over it again with the knife until it comes away with no effort. Push chunks out from the front; this way the fluffy edges won't be as noticeable. (If you are left with any fluff, however, slice it off with your knife.)

To cut through two pieces of paper at once requires a little more pressure. Remove cut-out chunks from the top layer as they're cut, but leave chunks from the bottom in place until you've cut out the whole pattern; they're unlikely to have been sliced properly, and won't come away cleanly. Go over them again until they do.

✂ *Cutting straight lines*
Always use a ruler, and be careful when you get to a corner; should you over-cut a line it will look far less professional, as below.

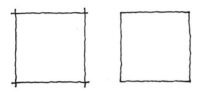

✂ *Cutting curves*
This is a two-handed operation: one cuts, the other rotates the paper. Do short curves with one swift cut, but for longer curves, break paper-cutting rules and stop midway to rest your hand, if needed. Or, invest in a set of metal French curves and match the tool up to the curve you need to cut.

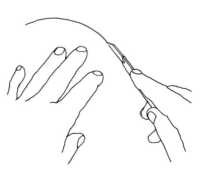

✂ *Symmetrical cuts*
If your pattern is a symmetrical one, fold the paper in half carefully, then slice through both bits at once.

COMMON PROBLEMS

My hand hurts. Time to change the blade; a blunt knife requires more pressure to cut. Give your hand a good shake and let it rest for a few minutes before you tackle the paper again.

Help! I've cut through the wrong bit of paper. Turn the page for some advice from a pro.

The masterclass

JONATHAN 'MR YEN' CHAPMAN
ON CUTTING OUT WORDS
FROM DR SEUSS QUOTES TO THE MOST DELICATE FEATHERS, THIS ARTIST CUTS MAGIC INTO EACH PIECE OF PAPER HE GETS HIS HANDS ON. *mr-yen.com*

IF YOU'RE CUTTING THE LETTERS OUT

'First, I decide if I want to keep the counters (the bits in the middles of the letters) or not: sometimes keeping these makes reading the words easier, sometimes the counters look best removed,' he says. Though instinctively we assume a capital 'A' should have that triangle in the middle, it can look more interesting and contemporary (and be easier) not to have it there. If you want to keep these counters, they must be attached to the main body of paper somehow; usually by leaving lines of paper that touch the counter and the main piece. 'The best place to position these attaching lines depends on the design or personal preferences,' he explains. 'When deciding the placement, you do need to consider the structure and strength of them.' A line just 0.5mm wide will be less sturdy than something 2mm wide, for example, and two lines will be stronger than one. Wherever you choose to position these lines, cut them in the same position for every letter: consistency looks professional.

IF YOU'RE CUTTING OUT THE SPACE AROUND THE LETTERS

'You have to consider things more carefully when creating a paper cut with negative space being cut out,' he says. 'A good rule is that each letter should touch at least one or two sections of your design. If it touches one, you know it will be intact in the final piece; if it touches two, you know the letter form will be held in position more securely.' In this instance, it's well worth putting the time in to sketch your paper cut first.

INSIDER TRICKS

'Yupo paper is really nice to cut through. It is made from 100 per cent recycled plastic, so the blade glides through it like butter, and it is tear-resistant as well.'

KATRINE HILDEBRAND, PAPER ARTIST

katrinehildebrandt.com

CLAIRE BREWSTER

ON BOUNCING BACK FROM A MISTAKE

IT'S A PAINSTAKING JOB TO HAND-CUT INTRICATE FLORA AND FAUNA FROM OLD MAPS AND ATLASES, BUT CLAIRE MAKES IT LOOK EFFORTLESS AND INCREDIBLY BEAUTIFUL: IT'S THE REASON HER WORK HAS BEEN EXHIBITED IN GALLERIES ACROSS THE WORLD. *clairebrewster.co.uk*

KEEP STICKY TAPE TO HAND

'First, don't panic. If you have simply made a cut in the wrong part of your paper, you can probably fix it with a little clear sticky tape. Turn it over so that the wrong side is facing up, mend it with a small piece of tape, and turn it back over. No one will ever know the difference.

THINK CREATIVELY

'If you've had a more drastic accident that tape won't mend without it being really noticeable (you have a large rip or have made a much bigger cut in the wrong place, for example), you will have to reassess your design, or start again. As it's a shame to waste all your hard work, it's always best to attempt to mend first. Can you add an extra heart/star/other shape? Can your heart/star/other shape be wider/longer/bigger?

CHANGE YOUR BLADE

'Accidents usually happen when you are trying to cut with a blunt knife: you apply more pressure, so you cut or rip bits that you didn't mean to.'

'When doing intricate cutting, it helps to lift your knife to the very tip of the blade at the end of a line to prevent over cutting.'

BOVEY LEE, PAPER ARTIST

boveylee.com

'Most people forget to cut in adequate light: remember, don't work in your own shadow.'

KRIS TRAPPENIERS, PAPER ARTIST

kristrappeniers.tumblr.com

'I always lean on a separate piece of paper while cutting so I don't rub out pencil marks or damage fragile pieces I've already cut.'

MIKE LOMAX, PAPER ARTIST

mjlomax.co.uk

The project

THE SIMPLE COFFEE TABLE

Restyle that identikit coffee table/bookshelf/set of drawers. Easy – and cheap.

HOW HARD IS IT TO DO?
As hard as you make it.

HOW LONG DOES IT TAKE?
An evening or two, depending how intricate your paper cut is (drying time is extra).

MATERIALS

1. Ikea coffee table or similar
2. Lace
3. Printer
4. Paper
5. Pencil
6. Craft knife
7. Cutting mat
8. Ruler
9. Spray mount
10. Newspaper
11. Clear polyurethane varnish
12. Brush

STEP 1
You could design a paper cut freehand, from scratch (it's a brilliant way to personalise furniture), but, if you're not confident doing something intricate, using a piece of lace as your base is a cracking way to get yourself a fancy pattern. Once you've found a piece you like, take a photo and use your computer to enlarge it. The size you enlarge it to depends on the size of the furniture you're decorating.

STEP 2
Print out your lace (you will probably have to print out sections on to a few pieces of A4 paper, then tape them together), then put it up to the table, to check it's the right size.

STEP 3
Now it's time to simplify your lace pattern. Draw over the top of it in pencil, following the rules on pages 130–132: make sure all shapes and pieces are attached to something, and if you think something will be über-difficult to cut neatly, make it less detailed. Draw over your final design in pen, or trace it on to a new sheet of paper.

STEP 4
Get yourself a flat surface and a cutting mat. Lay the simplified lace pattern on top of the paper and cut it (following all the safety precautions on page 130, of course).

STEP 5
All done? Excellent. Carefully turn over your paper cut and place it on top of a couple of sheets of newspaper (to protect your surfaces). Cover it with spray mount (which is basically glue in a can), and stick it in place on your coffee table. You'll have a minute or so to move it around before the glue sets; when you love the way it looks, smooth it down with the side of your hand.

STEP 6
Following the instructions on the side of the tin, give the entire table a couple of thin layers of varnish (do this within half a day of sticking the paper down).

The extras

CREATE A PERSONALISED PIECE OF ART

If you're going to slave over a paper cut for days, you might as well create something meaningful that you'll want to give pride of place. Cutting silhouettes of family and friends is a paper-cut classic: take a side-on photo of their head and neck, or a full-length shot from the front, print it out and cut out the person. Draw around this template on to a black, coloured or patterned piece of cut card and cut out. Paper-cut maps look excellent too, especially if you use one of your local area (place the map on top of your paper and carefully cut out all the roads), or you could cut those most cherished lines from a poem, song or book.

MAKE FRIENDS WITH THE OFFICE LAMINATOR

(Because no one actually owns one of these, do they?) Give your paper cuts strength by laminating them and you open up a wonderful new world of opportunity. (If you don't have access to a laminator, sandwich the paper in between two sheets of sticky-back plastic for a similar-ish effect). Punch a hole through the corner and you can use them as birthday present tags, Christmas decorations, pendants and earrings (yes, I do mean jewellery – just don't hang out in the rain too much). Or make large paper-cut triangles, laminate them, then staple them evenly along a piece of ribbon to make an alternative to fabric bunting.

LET THERE BE LIGHT

Find a glue that sticks paper to glass and attach your paper cut to the outside of a glass candleholder (or an old jam jar with a tea light inside): watch the dappled flame shine through. Or, make a paper cut from card, give it a coating of fire-retardant spray (on both sides, according to the instructions on the can) and wrap it around the frame of a lampshade. The easiest way to do this is to use a tubular shade frame, and cut the card so it's 4cm ($\frac{1}{2}$in) taller than the shade and 4cm longer than the diameter. Don't make any decorative cuts 4cm from the top or bottom edge, and make sure you don't cut out so much that it's not sturdy or lets out too much light. Lay the shade on its side and wrap the card around it, so 2cm ($\frac{3}{4}$in) sticks out over the top and bottom. Fold this 2cm over the top and bottom of the frame and secure with strong glue (a couple of pegs will hold the card in place while it dries).

EMBELLISH EVERYTHING

If it can be given a coat of varnish or covered in sticky-back plastic, you can decorate it with a paper cut (it's a bit like the 'single-image trick' in the Découpage chapter, on page 43). The front of a notepad or old book, a tin pencil case, the lid of a decorative box, a wooden bangle, the thick arms of a pair of sunglasses, a phone cover … be adventurous, of course, but don't forget to also be sensible. Embellish things because they'll look better because of it, not just for the sake of it.

MOVE ON FROM PAPER

Once you've mastered the cutting technique you can experiment with other materials. Self-adhesive vinyl is a favourite; you need to apply more pressure to cut it, but once you've cracked it, you can make your own wall stickers in no time, perfect for sprucing up rented flats without blowing your deposit (make sure the packaging confirms it doesn't leave marks on walls). Work on as big a cutting mat as you can get your hands on, and you could whip up a contemporary version of a Victorian ceiling rose, an ornate frame to stick around a cheap square mirror, or something large and unexpected: a line of pink flamingos, maybe? Fabrics that don't fray – leather or felt – are strong enough to hold their shape, too; rather than a craft knife, they can be cut with sewing scissors and appliquéd on to any fabric using oversew stitch (see page 211).

The great craft debate

Tracey Emin sews, so does my nana. My nana's stitching might take pride of place in my lounge, but Emin's work hangs in the finest galleries in the world and sells for six-figure sums. What's the difference? What makes some craft art and other craft, well, just craft?

'PEOPLE AREN'T AFTER MY SKILL; THEY WANT MY CREATIVITY'

Turner Prize-winning **Grayson Perry** is best known for his incredible, and controversial, ceramics and tapestries (and dressing as his alter-ego, Claire).

'When most people talk about "craft" they're talking about making Christmas cards with the kids. When I use that term I'm talking about medieval masons and lace-tapestry makers. Real craftspeople dedicate large portions of their lives to learning a skill and practising it.

'It would be a lie to say that I'm a craftsman, because I'm not defined by my skill. People aren't after my skill; they want my creativity. How involved I am in the actual making process depends entirely on the medium. With pottery I do everything, from mud to masterpiece. I design the tapestries in Photoshop and they're woven for me. I designed the motorbike [a mobile shrine to his childhood teddy bear], but all I made was a little sculpture for it to be based on, and the sculptures mounted to the front and in the shrine. I'm pragmatic about these things: I could learn to bend sheet metal and spend ten years mastering it so I could build the bike myself, but what if I didn't want to make another one? It's hardly practical.

'Pottery and tapestries have a resonance for me; when I started using them I was very aware of their seemingly lower status compared to something like painting. And I think that will always be an issue. The art world has to get over the naff suburban image that things like pottery and knitting have, whereas other techniques that have also been recently embraced, like video, don't have another mumsy version to contend with. But I think it's a false dichotomy, because painting is now just as much a craft as knitting or pottery; on the whole it's practised in the same very traditional way by fairly unimaginative people.

'It's up to the artist how creative they are with the techniques they use. I don't throw a batch of pots and then fire and glaze them like everyone else. I make a pot like a one-off three-dimensional painting, and have developed many of the techniques myself to just the kind of look I want.'

'I NEVER INTENDED TO BECOME AN ARTIST'

Kate Jenkins was a successful knitwear designer, creating patterns for everyone from Debenhams to Marc Jacobs, but now her own knitted designs can be found in London's Rebecca Hossack Art Gallery *(cardigan.ltd.uk)*.

'I don't like calling myself an artist; it doesn't feel right. Although the work I create now can be found in a frame in a gallery, just as much effort and passion went into the designs I created before. To me, knitwear is a piece of art, whether you wear it or find it behind a piece of glass. When people ask what I do I usually tell them that I make things out of wool. It's not that I'm embarrassed; it's just that I just never set out to be an artist; initially, I made the things that I now exhibit as publicity for my knitwear label, Cardigan.

'I spend half a year on my exhibitions and half on Cardigan. What's the difference between these two aspects of my work? Well, I design and make everything in the shows, but only design the homewares and accessories now. They are sold to people who live in very different worlds, too; the exhibited crochet goes to art collectors, and the Cardigan lines go to people who want affordable design for themselves and their home.

'I don't see much of a difference between art and craft. I think if you can make something of great quality that can be exhibited in a gallery and sells at gallery prices, it doesn't matter whether it's been made from wool or paint or ceramics. I'm sure some people think my work isn't "proper art" because it's made from crochet, but isn't all art subjective anyway?'

'IT'S LIKE CALLING A JIGSAW ART, BECAUSE YOU PUT ALL THE PIECES TOGETHER YOURSELF'

Rob Ryan's unique style of paper cut is instantly recognisable and found everywhere from galleries to the side of a mug *(misterrob.co.uk)*.

'For me, craft is based on instruction. It's like painting by numbers: you buy the pack, follow the instructions, and put the paint where the numbers are. I'm not saying it's not a great thing to do, but it's like calling a jigsaw art, because you put all the pieces together yourself.

'Craft stops becoming craft when people design it themselves. And once people have an idea and they put it into practice and they make it, then I don't think it can be considered craft anymore. There's no point in saying that what Tracey Emin does is craft because she uses stitches and blankets, for example. It's got nothing to do with the medium. It's to do with ideas and thought. Perhaps people are happier calling what they have created "craft" because they modestly don't deem it worthy of being called "art".

'That said, the lines between what is and what isn't art or craft or illustration or anything else is so blurred. The world is a changing place. One hundred years ago galleries exhibited oil paintings and sculptures made from marble or bronze. Now you go into galleries and there's neon and fabric and all sorts. But there's just as much bad art as there is bad craft, and across the UK there are just as many twenty-one-year-olds putting up bad art degree shows as there are old women putting bad craft up in church halls.

'I consider myself an artist, but I have been called a craftsman because I work with paper. I've also been called a graphic designer because I've done a book cover, and an illustrator because a couple of my pictures have been used in newspapers. At the end of the day, people will call you whatever they want. I just do what I enjoy. Whether that makes me a craftsperson or an artist or whatever, I don't know. I don't waste a lot of time thinking about it; I just get on with the work I love to create. At the end of the day, who gives a shit?'

PORTRAIT OF THE ARTIST: TRACEY EMIN EXPLAINS ...

'I make hundreds of drawings and I do paint but the reason why I work with fabric and sewing is because I'm naturally adept at it and I find it a very easy medium to transfer my emotional feelings into. Sewing has a warmth and an intimacy. Fabrics seem to resonate something. They already have an emotion to them. And a lot of my early works are made from my old clothes and fabrics that mean something to me. I still hold on to some of these tiny bits of fabric as if they were gold.

'I have never faced opposition for using traditional handicrafts. Somehow it's been amazingly easy. But I do know that, traditionally, textiles aren't as valued and are considered to be craft and this reflects itself in the marketplace. But that's not why I make my work.'

'TRUST YOUR GUT'

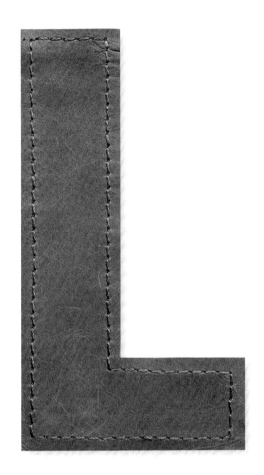

Leather work

Sure, it might look like yet another type of fabric, but be warned – leather is unlike any material you've ever sewn. Once you've learned the ropes, however, you'll soon be knocking together belts, bags and cuffs for everyone.

The technique

MATERIALS

1 Leather
Buy fake, buy real, buy cheap, buy pricey. Whatever you choose, the thicker it is, the harder it is to sew. How to know what quality and thickness of leather to choose? Investigate what similar products are made from and go from there.

2 Leather needle
This has a three-sided point, and is available for hand-sewing and for a sewing machine.

3 Thread
Avoid cotton. Strong polyester or nylon is fine for thin leather, but for anything really hefty, choose waxed linen thread.

4 Thimble

5 Masking tape, bulldog or paperclips, or hair grips
Anything but pins to hold two pieces of leather together for sewing. Pins leave unwanted, permanent holes.

6 Scissors/craft knife
If fabric scissors don't cut it, a sharp craft knife or leather shears will.

7 Teflon-plated sewing machine foot
A standard foot will suffice, but if you'll be doing a lot of leather work, invest in one of these, as it will glide over leather more smoothly.

8 Hammer and nail

GETTING STARTED

Use the real stuff and you should be prepared for a few blemishes (remember, leather does come from an animal). Check your hide before you buy, but don't automatically discard a piece just because of a few imperfections: can you cut a pattern around it? Fake leather doesn't have this issue, but looks, well, fake.

SEWING LEATHER

If you make a mistake on leather you can't just unpick it: your needle will have made irreparable holes. So whatever you craft, create templates from paper first to check your design works.

BY HAND

Stitching that will only be seen from one side can be done in a backstitch; don't pull the thread too tightly (otherwise you'll damage the leather) and keep your tension steady. Stitching that will be visible from both sides can't (one side would be neat, the other very messy). One method is to do a running stitch along the edge you need to sew, then using the same piece of thread, go back over your stitches with a running stitch again, filling in the blanks.

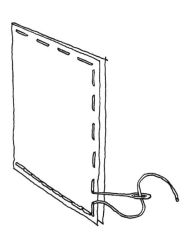

To secure the thread, use your needle to bring the end of it up between the two pieces of leather: tie a knot, then push it down with your needle so it can't be seen.

Alternatively, try a saddle stitch: a stronger, two-needle version of the above. Cut a long piece of thread, thread both ends with a needle, and poke one end through the two pieces of leather. Position the leather so it sits in the middle along the length of thread. Take the left needle and make a stitch. Poke the right needle through the same hole. Pull tight (but not too tight), and repeat all the way along the edge. Finish in the same way as the previous technique.

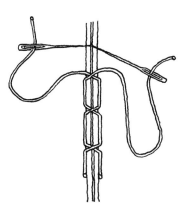

WITH A MACHINE

Or, let your sewing machine do the hard work. Using the appropriate needle and thread, set the machine to a long stitch and a low tension (if it's too tight the thread can cut through delicate leather) and always use the tying method (see page 18) to start and finish a line of stitching, so the knot sits between the two pieces of leather (the backstitch method of securing it will weaken the leather).

MAKING HOLES

Whether your holes are functional or decorative, you've got two ways to make them. Buy a leather punch and punch your heart out, or lay your leather right-side up on an old book, piece of wood or something equally hard (to protect your table), and use a hammer and nail to puncture it. As you remove the nail, twist it so it leaves a nice clean hole.

FINISHING OFF

Rough edges can be trimmed or buffed with fine sandpaper. Raw edges can be left as they are, or cut with special edging tools, dyed, or sealed with beeswax or similar products. (But, honestly, buying extra paraphernalia is only worth it if you *really* get into leather work.)

COMMON PROBLEMS

My leather is too thick to hand sew. No worries. Punch small holes at equal intervals where you want your line of stitching to be. Then you just have to pass the needle through them instead.

My needle has got goo all over it. If you've used sticky tape to hold two pieces of leather together, when you sew over it residue will be left on your needle. Just give it a good clean.

The masterclass

THE CAMBRIDGE SATCHEL COMPANY
ON KEEPING IT CONTEMPORARY

JULIE DEANE'S ICONIC, BRITISH-MADE SATCHELS HAVE A CULT CELEBRITY FOLLOWING. SHE HAS COLLABORATED WITH THE LIKES OF COMME DES GARÇONS AND ASOS, AND HER BAGS HAVE APPEARED IN FASHION GLOSSIES ACROSS THE WORLD. *cambridgesatchel.co.uk*

COLOUR IS KING

'I see a tremendous beauty in colour,' she says. 'If you have an incredible colour coupled with the perfect design, then that's very exciting.' Should your local fabric shop have a poor selection of coloured leather, try the internet for specialist sellers.

TINY DETAILS MATTER

'Sometimes, something just as subtle as changing the colour of the thread can make a huge difference. If a bag is going to look too drab we tend to use a contrasting thread for the stitching. When it follows the contours, it makes it really pop out.' Alternatively, she says, use two different-coloured leathers to create one item, and match the thread to the other colour to pull it all together.

DON'T SCRIMP ON QUALITY

'Leather is not a manmade textile. Animals have scars and marks and so some flaws are completely unavoidable.' But, she advises, buy better-quality skin and you're sure to get fewer marks; it's actually better value, because more of the fabric is usable. You should cut your pattern pieces in such a way that no marked leather is used: 'As the leather softens and wears, where the mark is, the material will become weaker.'

DESIGN, DESIGN AND DESIGN AGAIN

Leather is a pricey fabric, so it's not something you can afford to mess around with. 'It's important to feel passionate enough about your design that you can't wait to see it made,' she advises. 'You can't think "Oh, well, I think this will be OK. I'll make one and then see how I can improve it." You need to get to that stage where you're panting to get it finished.'

INSIDER
TRICKS

NAT THAKUR

ON MASTERING LEATHER WORK

THE FORMER MULBERRY AND GHOST LEATHER DESIGNER
NOW HAS HER OWN RANGE OF HIGH-END LEATHER PIECES;
HER PURSES RESEMBLE GIANT COINS AND, ON FIRST
GLANCE, HER MOST WELL-KNOWN COLLECTION OF BAGS
LOOKS LIKE THROW-AWAY GROCERY OR SWEET SHOP BAGS.
natthakur.com

SAVE THE ADVENTURES FOR LATER

'Start with something very simple that requires no
sewing at all – a key ring or a belt. Get a feel for the
material and how to cut it first,' she suggests. 'You have
to really understand leather, and the specific skin you're
working with before you start pushing boundaries.'
But have no fear, she says. 'Try not to be scared of it.
Leather can try to take control of you, but you have
to take control of the material. Don't be too precious
about it.'

MOCK-UPS ARE THE WAY FORWARD

'Make as many prototypes as possible before you make
the final piece,' she says, so that you don't make silly
mistakes and waste precious leather. 'I sometimes use
leatherette instead of fabric because it has more similar
properties to leather. Fabric can be very, very flimsy,
but with leatherette you've got the strength that leather
has. You can apply varnishes and colours to it, too.'
It's tempting to dive straight in, but in this instance,
you really shouldn't.

'If you can get to grips with a thimble, it will save your fingers,
and eventually make your stitching much neater. But you must
get a thimble that fits! They come in all different sizes, so make
sure it's quite tight.'

ZOE LARKINS, CREATOR OF HETTY AND DAVE LEATHER ACCESSORIES

love from hettyanddave.co.uk

'When you work with very thick cowhide, the sewing
machine teeth can scratch it. To combat this I place
greaseproof paper under the leather to protect it, and sew
as normal. After, the paper can be easily torn away.'

NNEKA ONYENAKALA, FOUNDER AND DESIGNER OF
N'DAMUS LONDON

ndamus.com

The project

THE LEATHER NOTEBOOK COVER

So you can't afford a Smythson diary? That's OK. With this reusable leather cover, any old notepad or diary can look smashing.

HOW HARD IS IT TO DO?

The stitching is tricky, but with practice it will get easier.

HOW LONG DOES IT TAKE?

Set aside a Sunday morning.

MATERIALS

1   Notebook (BOUND, NOT A RINGBINDER)

2   Paper

3   Pencil

4   Leather (BETWEEN 0.8 AND 1MM THICK)

5   Tailor's chalk

6   Metal ruler

7   Craft knife

8   Thread

9   Leather needle

10 Hair grips or other fastener

11 Zipper machine foot (OPTIONAL)

12 Tracing paper/ greaseproof paper

STEP 1

Measure the height, width and depth of your notebook: from these measurements you can make a template. (Do this on paper first, so you don't waste any expensive leather.) The height of the template is the height of your notebook, plus 10mm. The length is width + width + depth + two-thirds of the width + two-thirds of the width. For example, if a notebook is 210mm high, 148mm wide and 12mm deep, the template would measure 220mm by 712mm. Wrap this around your notebook to check it fits nicely.

STEP 2

It does? Wonderful. With the leather facing right-side down, draw around the template with tailor's chalk. Cut this out with a metal ruler and craft knife (this gives the leather a cleaner edge than scissors). Do it slowly and carefully: spend time getting this right as neat edges are what makes the end result look most professional.

STEP 3

At this point it's worth cutting a small piece of leather from your hide to test. Whether you're using a machine or sewing by hand, get comfortable stitching it before you move on to the real thing.

STEP 4

Wrap your leather around the notebook to check it fits (and to ensure the same amount of leather is folded over the front and back covers). Before you sew you might like to embellish the front with stitches, punched holes or otherwise. Or, like I did, you could leave it plain.

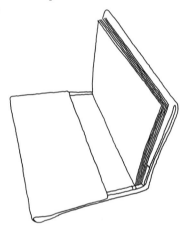

STEP 5

Without unfolding the leather, whip out the notebook (do it slowly, one side at a time, and it is possible). Use hair grips or similar to hold the folds in place.

STEP 6

Now it's time to sew around the edge of the cover, 3mm from the edge. Use whichever of the two hand stitches on page 143 you feel

happier with, or use your machine (remember, the top stitch has to go on top, so your leather must be right side up as you stitch). Change to a leather needle and add a zipper foot (if you have one – it means you can easily line up the edge of the foot to the edge of the leather to get the neatest possible stitching). Put a piece of tracing or greaseproof paper in between the machine and the leather, so the teeth don't make any marks.

STEP 7

Start sewing where the black dot is on the illustration below.

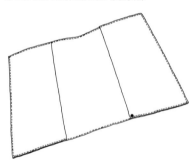

If you can do the whole thing in one go, great – there'll be fewer knots to contend with. But don't fret if you can't. If your machine struggles to go through the leather, try turning it off and using the wheel manually to move the needle up and down to create the stitches. The four corners are going to be the trickiest when using a machine, so aim to finish a stitch a couple of millimetres from the edge. Keep the needle down, in the leather; by doing this you can rotate the cover, moving it into a new position to stitch the next edge.

You're almost done. (If you've used a machine, now is the time carefully to rip off the greaseproof paper.) If the top and bottom edges of your cover look wonky, you can smarten them up with a metal ruler and a craft knife. Just be sure not to slice through any stitches.

Fold the front and back cover of your notebook back as far as they will go without breaking, then slip your new cover on. If it's a really snug fit, take it slowly so as not to put too much pressure on the stitches.

'DESIGN, DESIGN AND DESIGN AGAIN'

The extras

PUT SCRAPS TO GOOD USE

Don't waste expensive leather scraps; here are a few projects to use up offcuts. To make simple but classy earrings, punch a hole in a diamond-shaped piece, slip a jump ring through and attach it to an earring hook (as page 180). Key rings are made in a similar way, but to make them as sturdy as possible, cut two of the same shape (remember to flip the template over for the second piece) and sew together, wrong sides facing. Or, appliqué scraps of leather on to something already made of leather to add depth and texture (page 212). Cover a small piece in embroidery and glue a brooch pin to the back. Sew a press stud on to either end of a very long strip and wrap it around your wrist three or four times for a bracelet. Or, to make a headband, sew each end of a short strip to the end of a piece of elastic so it makes a loop.

A LOVELY LEATHER CUFF

This is a cracking little gift for a male or female friend. All you need is a set of press studs and a strip of leather. The strip should be long enough to fit around their wrist and then be cut about 2cm (³⁄₄in) longer, and be between 3cm (1in) and 8cm (3in) wide. Use a lovely, decorative leather or a plain, but good-quality piece and you can leave it at that.

However, if you like things a little more embellished, get busy with embroidery (page 28), encrusting (page 68), or throw on a few studs (page 20). A few carefully placed holes punched in your strip can look brilliant, too. To finish, sew on your press studs neatly (remember, you'll be able to see the back of your stitching when you're wearing it).

A SLOUCHY LEATHER CLUTCH

The thicker the leather, the sturdier your clutch will be. Cut a rectangle and lay it on a flat surface. Fold up the bottom edge of the leather by at least two-thirds, crease it and keep it in place with hair grips. Stitch up both sides, 2mm in from the edge, and you're almost done! Fold the top edge over to make a flap, and add a few press studs. Sandwich it between two heavy books before you use it, so it keeps its shape.

DIY GADGET HOLDER

Because a fancy phone or tablet needs a fancy case. Cut two pieces of leather just bigger than your gadget (make a paper template first to work out how big each piece needs to be). Use hair grips to hold the pieces together, wrong sides facing, and sew around the two long edges and one short side. Make it look polished by rounding off the bottom corners of the leather with scissors before you sew. Passport holders, train ticket holders, even sunglasses cases can be made using a similar method; just adapt the size of the pieces to fit. And if you're worried that this style of case isn't secure enough, no sweat: make one using the same method as the slouchy leather clutch, opposite.

ALL BELTED UP

A deceptively simple project. Find a buckle you love (buy one new from a haberdashery or cut one from an old belt) and use a belt you already wear to work out how long your strip of leather needs to be. To attach a traditional buckle (the ones with a prong), use a nail or punch to add a hole about 5cm (2in) from one end of the strip. Then, poke the buckle's prong through it, and fold the end of the leather strip over so that the wrong sides touch each other. Stitch in place as neatly and securely as possible (examine how other belts look if you get stuck). At the other end of the strip, punch a series of holes at equal intervals (again, use an old belt as a template) and you've got yourself a nice new belt.

All things weird and wonderful

The world of craft occasionally serves up an unexpected treat: a knitted Harry Potter, an embroidered Lady Gaga, an origami David Cameron, and much, much more. Great, but why would anyone bother making something like that?

Search for the cult vampire novel *Twilight* on Etsy and you get a staggering 14, 563 hits. The world's biggest handmade marketplace is awash with screen-printed Team Edward T-shirts, Bella-inspired jewellery and – surely everyone's favourite – the hand-painted dummy that makes your baby look like it has vampire fangs. Here, as on blogs, forums and Flickr, crafters immortalise every last detail of the vampire/werewolf/human three-way in quilts, cross stitch and everything in between.

Such extreme, crafty devotion from fans is nothing new (*Doctor Who* fans have been knitting the iconic Tom Baker scarf since the 1970s) and it's certainly not limited to cult fantasy novels. As you wander through the internet it won't be long before you stumble on some kind of fan craft: the embroidered face of Obama, Cheryl Cole made from sticky tape and matchsticks, the entire Arsenal squad made from paper. The dedication that goes into creating these replicas is astounding and admirable, if not – dare I say it – a little peculiar.

THE INVESTIGATION BEGINS
However, I like to think of myself as non-judgmental and open-minded, so rather than writing a snarky feature about People Who Make Strange Things straight off, I thought it best to at least pay a visit to the world of fan craft first. Don't say I never do anything for you…

The question that begs to be asked first is: why? If you're not making it for an eleven-year-old child, then what's with the Harry Potter quilt? If you're not bereft of friends or fun, why painstakingly recreate Lady Gaga's most iconic outfits for a line-up of Barbie dolls? I must admit that I've always assumed it was either a filling-the-endless-spare-time-I-have thing, or being a bit of a show-off. (Post a picture of your fan craft online and it screams; 'Look how much of a hardcore fan I am. I just spent 72 hours carving Britney Spears' face into a stone.')

It seems I'm much mistaken. 'It's more of a community than a competition,' **Susan Beal**, the author of *World of Geek Craft (westcoastcrafty.com)*, tells me. 'People are more likely to feel inspired or impressed by someone else's fan craft than feel one-upped.' She's not the only one who denies my (perhaps overly cynical) assumptions. **Jennifer Ofenstein**, founder of the FandomInStitches.com blog, says it has nothing to do with showing off, and everything to do with being a member of a community. 'It's part of the human experience to want to be part of something bigger,' she explains. She talks passionately about her fan-craft community – even likening it to a large, extended family – and firmly believes that making something based on a film or a novel or something else helps her to 'feel connected to other people who love the stories I love'.

And there's more. 'Creating something that celebrates the stories and people we love, whether real or fictional, is a way to remember what we felt at that moment,' Jennifer adds. Actually, she makes a lot of sense: who doesn't dread the last page of a great book, or the last song of that incredible gig, knowing once it comes, the magic is all over? You can replay it time and time again, of course, but it's never quite the same. Perhaps fan crafters are more canny than the rest of us: they don't rely on the inevitably bad sequel for their next fix; they stride right in there and make some follow-up magic themselves.

It doesn't explain everything, though, else surely we'd see *Grease/Die Hard/Rocky*-themed makes popping up across the web. But we don't. *Star Wars*, *Star Trek*, *Twilight*, *Harry Potter*, *Lord of the Rings* – these are the stories being stitched. Again, Jennifer has some interesting insights. 'Any story that resonates with people, that creates a strong emotional reaction, that fills a void, that hits a cultural nerve, is one that will see art and crafts to follow.' That certainly explains as well why there's such a culture of craft in sci-fi and fantasy worlds, and explains the raft of Obama and Lady Gaga craft too. (It almost justifies that thin sliver of JLS fan craft as well. No scoffing in the back there.) And any story that fires up your imagination can expect to get crafted. 'The world that JK Rowling created, even before the movies existed, is so fascinating that it screams to be re-explored by the reader,' she says. Susan agrees; anything that is extremely visual, she adds, translate beautifully to craft.

THE JOKE'S ON US?

Actually, it's much harder to mock this stuff after hearing from these ladies. (I'd half expected to find them basement-bound, madly crafting wands in case Daniel Radcliffe dropped by wanting to play wizards.) But they are just normal, regular people. I still can't help myself, though – are they the exception rather than the rule? Definitely not, Jennifer says. 'There's no "type" per se, unless "enthusiastic" and "creative" are types.' (Which is understandable: should every fan take a detour via John Lewis' haberdashery after every *Twilight* screening, we'd have a worldwide shortage of black and red felt.) And as Susan reminds me, there really are levels of fandom: the person who makes a Madonna-themed birthday card for a friend will be somewhat different to the person who flies halfway across the world to a Madonna gig dressed in a cardboard replica of the 'Like a Virgin' cone bra.

Interestingly, while I ask about the fans as if they're some kind of rare, peculiar species, Susan actually questions why more of us aren't doing it. 'This era is so defined by popular culture, so many of us are watching the same shows, cheering on the same teams, or reading the same books, and lots of us also enjoy making things for fun, so the crossover potential is pretty amazing,' she says. 'If you're skeptical, fair enough, but if you like to make things, and you're a fan of something – a soccer team, or a political party, or a TV series – why not make an inspired craft project and share it online, and with friends who appreciate it, too. The response you get might surprise you.' She makes a fair point. Maybe *I'm* the Person Who Makes Strange Things after all …

'TINY
DETAILS
MATTER'

Macramé

*Once considered the height of naffness, macramé –
the art of knotting – has been revived by a
new generation of fashion designers who have
taken it on to the catwalk and brought it back
to the high street.*

The technique

MATERIALS

1 Cord

Hemp, sisal, jute and other natural materials are typically used because they're so sturdy. However, they also give macramé that 1970s hanging basket look, so I recommend avoiding them in favour of cord made from leather, cotton or suede instead. Even thin ribbon or thick thread could work; anything that looks luxurious.

2 A base

Anything long and thin that you can tie cord to, such as a pencil, knitting needle or chopstick.

3 Masking tape

GETTING STARTED

Cut a length of cord/string/whatever ten times as long as you want your finished piece to be. Fold it in half. Poke the two ends through the looped end of the cord and slip it on to a pencil or stick. Use a couple of strips of masking tape to fix the pencil to a table surface in front of you so you don't have to hold it.

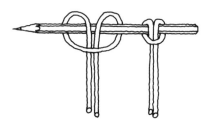

THE KNOTS

I know it looks complicated, but macramé is just a series of ornamental knots; you learn a few, then combine them in any number of ways to create something marvellous. Here are a few of the most basic and versatile.

A HALF HITCH

Tie a cord to a pencil, then simply wrap one strand around the other and through the loop, as illustrated. Do it again and you've got yourself a double half hitch.

HALF SQUARE KNOT

Tie two cords on to a pencil as above, so you have four strands. Take the right cord over the two middle ones, and under the left one. Poke the left one through that little gap from the back as below, and – keeping the middle cords in the same position – pull the ends of the left and right cord slowly to tighten.

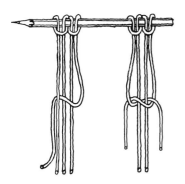

SQUARE KNOT

Make a half square knot. Now, take the right cord under the two middle ones and over the left one.

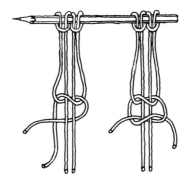

Poke the left-hand one through that gap from the front, and gently pull the ends of the left and right cords to finish, again making sure the middle cords stay straight.

MACRAMÉ PATTERNS

Some are simple, the others mind-bogglingly complex. These are a few I like …

- ✂ *A spiral:* make a series of half-square knots and you'll soon transform four strands into a pretty twist.

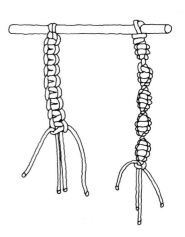

- ✂ *A bar:* a line of square knots creates this stylish length of macramé.

✂ *A square row:* tie 8, 12, 16 (or any number divisible by four) strands to a pencil, and tie square knots all the way along the line (the first knot from strands 1–4, the second with 5–8, and so on). For the next row, ignore the first two strands, then tie another line of square knots (strands 3–6, 7–10, etc.). Repeat these two rows.

✂ *A half-hitch row:* tie an even number of strands on, and work a row of double half hitches.

✂ *An arrow:* made using an even number of strands. Bring the first strand across the first half of the strands and tie double half hitches to it, diagonally. Repeat with the last strand, until you've made your arrow. Make two arrows and you get a diamond.

FINISHING OFF

When you're happy with your macramé, tie a standard knot in each strand to stop it unravelling (the one you tie in the end of a piece of sewing thread). Trim the cords just under this knot, so they're all the same length, or keep them long for a tassel effect.

COMMON PROBLEMS

My long strands keep getting tangled. Try wrapping the ends around a piece of card, or tying them in a little bundle with an elastic band.

The ends of my cord are unravelling. Dip them in a clear-drying glue or clear nail varnish and allow to dry.

INSIDER TRICKS

'Practise new knots in neutral, but contrasting colours, in a cord that is soft to handle and easy to manipulate. When I started I used rat-tail cord, which is soft, retains its shape well when knotted, and unknots easily if you make a mistake.'

GINA MARRIS, MACRAMÉ ARTIST

folksy.com/shops/Gmade

The masterclass

ELEANOR AMOROSO
ON COUTURE MACRAMÉ

THIS YOUNG DESIGNER'S FRESH TAKE ON AN OLD-FASHIONED CRAFT HAS DELIGHTED THE WORLD OF FASHION. *eleanoramoroso.com*

INVESTIGATE THE HABERDASHERY SHOP
'Find a material that is available in long lengths and isn't traditionally used for macramé. I use fringing, but you could use wool or thread, too; you will find plenty of options in a haberdashery.

STICK TO NEUTRALS
'I use a lot of black and cream to keep my work looking elegant and modern. Coloured strands can look quite tacky if you're not careful, and using any kind of colour can definitely look more "crafty".

BEADS DON'T HAVE TO LOOK NAFF
'In macramé you can slip beads on to your thread before you knot it. I wanted to use beading in my first collection, but the garments were so big I had to find some with large-enough holes; I ended up using metal piping from a DIY shop. Using unusual things like this stop macramé from looking dated.

DON'T BE AFRAID TO FREESTYLE
'I use the traditional macramé knots, but tend to adapt them as I go along. I might look at a pattern for inspiration, but I always work from scratch and build up combinations of knots as I work. Beautiful macramé is all about the way in which you put the individual knots together.

DON'T GIVE UP
'Macramé seems really complicated when you begin, but once you've done it for a little while it's something you quickly get the hang of. Just be patient; anything large will take a long time to create.'

'I like to recycle, so I use plastic bags as cord. Cut them into long, thin strips and knot them together, to make one long strip of yarn.'

LAURA LANG DIX, MACRAMÉ ARTIST

jennydebode.ning.com/profile/LauraLangDix

'I find 1mm braided nylon cord is best. To seal endless knots, you simply put it near the flame of a tea light, hold it for two seconds, and press it with your thumb to flatten.'

LAURA SNELL, MACRAMÉ ARTIST

etsy.com/people/JapanFan

The project

THE HANDY PURSE

Call it a purse, call it a make-up bag, call it a pencil case; whatever you use it for, these little zipped bags are super-handy. And when made in jewel colours with a splash of macramé, they look more glamorous than usual handmade fare.

HOW HARD IS IT TO DO?
Don't let the zip scare you; the only skill you need is to be able to sew in a straight line.

HOW LONG DOES IT TAKE?
A couple of hours.

MATERIALS

1 Fabric

2 Tailor's chalk

3 Ruler

4 Scissors

5 Iron

6 Zip

7 Pins

8 Needle

9 Thread

10 Zipper foot

11 Thin ribbon (ROPE OR OTHER MACRAMÉ MATERIAL)

STEP 1
You're going to need four rectangles of fabric, all the same size; how big they are depends on how long your zip is (there's a tutorial for how to shorten a zip on page 196–7). These instructions are based on a 20cm (8in) zip. Cut four pieces, 20cm by 15cm (8in by 6in): two of these will make up the outside of the purse, two will become the lining. Do you want your lining a different colour? Maybe you want the front and back to each be a different colour? Mix it up however you like.

STEP 2
Cut two more rectangles, 3cm by 6cm (1¼in by 2½in), from the fabric you used for the outside (the short edge is always the width of the zip, the long edge is always double that number). Fold each piece in half (so they are 3cm by 3cm/1¼in square) and iron to set the crease. These will become zip-guards that hide the untidy ends of the zip.

STEP 3
Don't turn the iron off just yet, as you need to fold over the long, top edge of your four rectangles by 1cm (½in). Iron the creases in place.

(CONTINUED OVERLEAF)

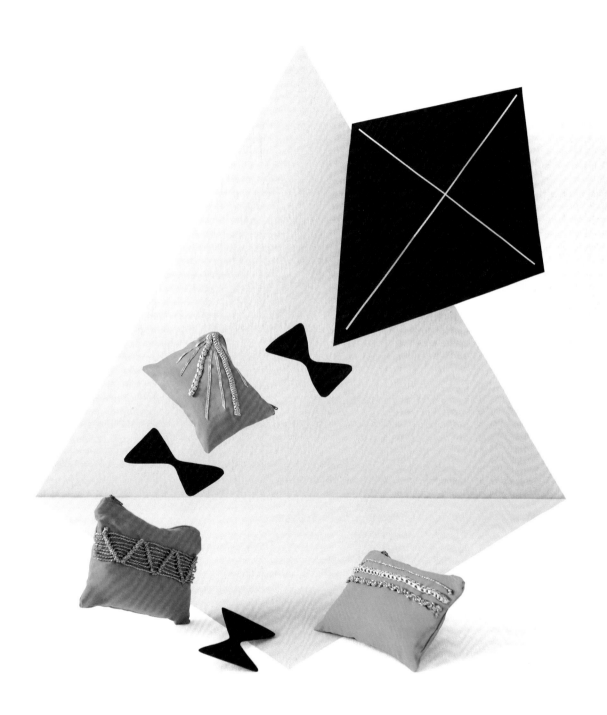

STEP 4

Now it's time to make what is best described as a zip sandwich. Lay the two lining pieces wrong side up, 1cm (½in) away from each other (their folded edges nearest each other).

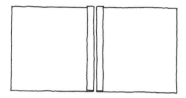

Place the zip on top, teeth facing up. Those two little rectangles – the zip guards – that you made earlier come into play now: lay them on top of the zip at either end. The unfolded edge should line up with the edge of the lining fabric.

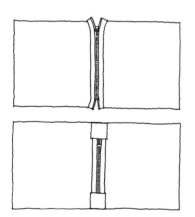

Finally, put the two outer pieces directly on top of the lining pieces, right-side up. (Again, the long folded edge goes over the zip). Pin everything together.

STEP 5

Two lines of stitching are all you need to keep the zip sandwich in place; these go either side of the zip, 2mm from the edge of the fabric. If you're hand sewing, use a backstitch. If you've got a machine, crack out your zipper foot (you can align this with the edge of the fabric and so stitch a super-neat straight line).

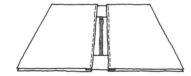

STEP 6

At last! You can finally get around the macramé malarkey. Make lengths of macramé – as simple or as complex as you fancy – and stitch them on to the outer piece of your purse. (Use the same colour of thread as your macramé material not the fabric.) Remember, you'll lose 1cm all the way around the edge when you sew the pieces together, so I recommend not covering these parts with macramé.

STEP 7

Make sure your zip is two-thirds open at this point. (You can tell this part is really important because it has its own step.)

STEP 8

Your next job is to fold your fabric in such a way that the outer pieces face each other and the lining pieces face each other. And, you must position the zip tape and zip guards so that they are folded on the lining side. Pin everything together so you're ready to sew. (I must just check – your zip is definitely still two-thirds open, right?)

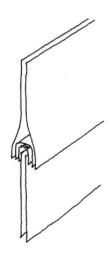

STEP 9

Using a backstitch, sew all the way around the edge of the rectangles, 1cm from the edge, but leave about 10cm (4in) unstitched on the lining.

STEP 10

Cut the corners of your rectangles (on both the outer pieces and the lining) a couple of millimetres or so from the edge of the stitching. This makes it easier for you to get crisp corners.

STEP 11

At the moment, your purse is inside out. Use the hole you left in the lining to turn it the right way around. (You remember I was really strict about you leaving the zip two-thirds open? This is why. If you hadn't, it would be near impossible to do this.) You should be left with something that looks like a purse spewing out its lining.

STEP 12

Now is an excellent time to poke the bottom two corners of your purse carefully, so the corners are nice and, well, corner-y. You should also poke the top two corners out gently, too, so that zip-guard is as angular as possible. (Put your hand inside the lining if that helps.)

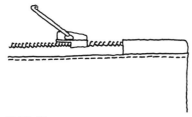

STEP 13

Oversew (see page 18) the hole you left in the lining, then neatly push it all into the purse. And you are, finally, ready to fill it up.

The extras

KNOT YOURSELF
A NECKLACE

Get macramé jewellery wrong
and it'll look like you're wearing a
friendship bracelet from the 1990s,
but get it right and you're sure to
make a statement. Knot a spiral or
bar (see page 157) long enough to
wrap around your wrist three, five or
even seven times. Or make several
different lengths, all long enough to
go around your neck: slip the end of
each length through a large jump
ring (see page 180) and the other
ends to a second jump ring. Add a
clasp (see page 180) and you've got
yourself a chunky necklace. A short
length of macramé can be tied on
to a key ring (a simple present for a
bloke), or could be slipped on to a
jump ring and used as an earring or
necklace pendant.

A NEW TYPE OF
EMBELLISHMENT

In the same way that you would use
lace or another decorative trim, stitch
strips or patches of macramé on to
the cuffs or collars of a top, down
the front of a dress, or around the
neck of a jumper (take a look at the
catwalk for inspiration: macramé
is increasingly seen in couture
collections these days). A single strip
could be sewn on to a hairband or
the strap of a shoe, or you could
cover the side of a clutch with lengths
of macramé. Make sure you use a
matching thread, and stitch through
the holes in the knots.

GO LARGE

Once you get confident (or have a
lot of time on your hands), why not
consider making something bigger:
a belt, a bag, a scarf, or perhaps even
a top. You could freestyle shapes,
as Eleanor does, but I reckon it's
much easier to work with squares
of macramé and sew/knot them
together. Be sure to use as thick a
rope/wool/leather as you can get your
hands on, otherwise you'll still be
knotting into next year …

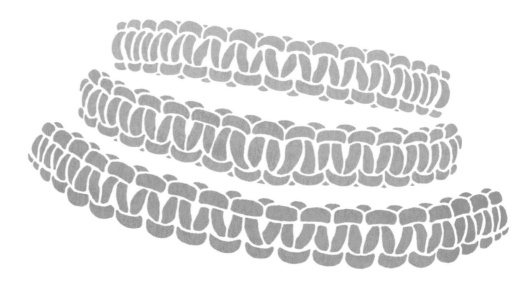

And the award goes to ...

Those people who champion craft in films, TV, books and interviews deserve a little recognition, don't you think? Think of this as a crafting Oscars, albeit without the statues, prize money or respect.

The Marmite award for dividing the world of craft

Whether you think she's the saviour of modern craft or an impostor who hijacked your hobby just as house prices were falling, you can't deny that the Channel 4 star Kirstie Allsopp gets us talking about what constitutes good making.

Best use of offensive crafting

Congrats to Judi Dench, who scoops this award for a brilliant handmade gift to playwright David Hare. To make up for a lousy set of reviews for his 1997 play 'Amy's View', she made him an embroidered cushion that said 'Fuck 'em, fuck 'em, fuck 'em, fuck 'em.' What. A. Legend.

The Katie Price award for ubiquitous crafting

Stateside, it has to be Julia Roberts, who hasn't given an interview in the last decade where she hasn't mention her love of craft. But let's not forget British actress Keeley Hawes of *Spooks*/ Boots No. 7 fame, who also manages to shoe-horn making into every available interview slot she can. Excellent work, ladies.

Most effective use of craft equipment in a non-crafting situation

It's 1978, it's Halloween, and Michael Myers is coming at you. Fair play, Jamie Lee Curtis, for grabbing a knitting needle and stabbing it into his neck. (See? That's why we're not allowed to craft on aeroplanes.)

Best celebrity contribution to Etsy

Mad Men's Christina Hendricks would have got this for her stellar performance modelling scarves for a friend's Etsy shop, had it not been for Courtney Love's ridiculous love/hate relationship with the handmade marketplace. Though she has a turbulent history with the site (having been sued for libel by one of the sellers after a super-extreme online rant about her), she still has a profile on the site and a list of favourites, which at one time included a portrait of herself and a glass-painted syringe.

Musical Services to Craft

That accolade must go to Gabby Young, front woman of folk/jazz/pop band Gabby Young and Other Animals. You'll find a haberdashery at most of her gigs (called the Gabberdashery, obviously), complete with handmade goods she has handpicked from her favourite designers. Kudos.

The Lifetime Achievement Award

She's after an internship with hat designer Philip Treacy. She put a sewing machine on her rider at Radio 1's Big Weekend. She showed kids how to craft with glitter at a special Thanksgiving show for US TV station ABC. It is, of course, Lady Gaga.

'DON'T
GIVE
UP'

Patchwork

Because the one thing that makes us smile more than a piece of beautiful material is ten different pieces of beautiful material stitched together.

The technique

MATERIALS

1 Fabric

100 per cent cotton is easiest to work with, stretchy fabrics are the most difficult, but essentially you can use anything. Fat quarters and charm squares are pre-cut patchworking fabrics; they save you cutting time, but are pricier.

2 Multi-purpose cotton thread

Use a complimenting colour to your fabric. Or go for grey, as it stands out less than white.

3 Pins

4 Fabric scissors

5 Ruler and dressmaking chalk

6 Iron

LUXURIES

1 Sewing machine

Because this will sew seams quicker. You could buy a specialist patchworking foot, but it's not vital.

2 Rotary cutter, self-healing mat and acrylic ruler

Use a complementing colour to your fabric. Or go for grey, as it stands out less than white.

GETTING STARTED

Hardcore quilters wash their fabric before stitching, in case it shrinks or excess colour runs out of it. I reckon it's only worth doing if your finished piece will ever have to go in the washing machine. Just make sure you iron it.

CUTTING IT UP

The simplest patchwork is created with squares of exactly the same size. Using a homemade cardboard template or shop-bought plastic one is the traditional method: lay it on the wrong side of the fabric, draw around, then cut out a zillion times.

How big should each square be? That depends; how big do you want the final piece of patchwork to be? Do you want it made up from loads of tiny pieces or a handful of large squares? Remember to allow for seams on all sides of each square (for some reason, $1/4$inch seams, not 5mm, are standard in patchwork. It's not vital if you're hand sewing, but a patchwork machine foot won't work properly if your seam isn't $1/4$ inch). Squares shouldn't be stretchy, so don't cut them on the bias.

PIECING THEM TOGETHER

Mix up squares randomly, or position them in a special sequence according to colour or pattern. Take a photo, so you'll have something to refer to if the squares get mixed up.

Work on the top line of pieces first. Pin the first two squares together, right sides facing (make sure they line up exactly), and backstitch together, ¼ inch from the edge. (To use a machine patchwork foot, line up the edge of the fabric with the edge of the foot). Take it slowly: if your seam is even 1mm out it'll make it more difficult to sew up later.

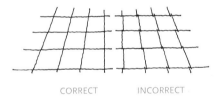

CORRECT   INCORRECT

Attach each piece this way until you have one long line of squares, and repeat for each line you have.

Now to iron the seams. Take the iron off the steam setting and press each seam to one side, so it is pushed flat against the back of the fabric.

On your top row, iron all the steams so they face one way, and on the next, iron them the other way.

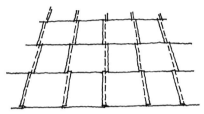

This is the trickiest bit. Pin the top row of squares to the second, right sides facing, and sew together with backstitch, ¼ inch from the edge. In an ideal world your squares will line up. Sew the other rows together and iron the seams as before. And that's it! Use your piece of patchwork just as you'd use any other piece of fabric – to make bags, clothes, cushions, or whatever takes your fancy.

DON'T BE SQUARE

There are infinite possibilities when it comes to patchwork design, but here are a few basics …

✄ *Sew rectangles just as you would squares.* Try using shapes that are twice as long as they are tall, and alternating rows of them sewn standing up and on their sides.

✄ *Triangles get sewn up like squares, too,* but inevitably one side will always be cut on the bias, making the pieces stretchy and more difficult to work with.

✄ *The classic harlequin pattern* is made up of rows of diamond shapes. Rather than sewing the top line of diamonds together, sew the top-right slant of one to the bottom-left slant of another, and so on. These form your 'lines'. (Or, the cheat's method is to make a square quilt and rotate it 45 degrees!)

COMMON PROBLEMS

My squares don't line up. You didn't sew your seams super-accurately like I told you to. Unpick it if it bothers you that much, or chalk this one down to experience and do better next time.

The masterclass

MICHAEL VAN DER HAM

ON MAKING CLASHING WORK

THE FASHION WORLD HAS FALLEN IN LOVE WITH THIS DUTCH DESIGNER. HIS LONDON FASHION WEEK COLLECTIONS ARE MADE UP OF MISMATCHED, PATCHWORKED GARMENTS THAT CLASH COMPLETELY BUT STILL LOOK INCREDIBLY SOPHISTICATED. *michaelvanderham.com*

EMBRACE THE CLASH

'The colours I use differ every season, but I think it always looks great to have a pastel next to a really bright colour; it works because one's really vivid and the other is really washed out,' Michael reveals. Fabrics should clash in texture and style as well as colour. 'In my first collection there weren't really any rules, other than if one section was metallic, no other section could be.' And maybe in price too. 'I would go to a place and buy fabric for £70 or £100 a metre, then get on the bus to Walthamstow and buy fabric for a pound a metre. But I didn't just go for cheap fabrics because they were cheap, I went for them because they were synthetic; they were a little edgier, because the drape of polyester crêpe is more severe than an expensive silk jersey.'

FORGET TRADITION

'I didn't want it all to be just patchworked,' he explains. 'Loads of it was also layered and draped.' Michael's use of texture, three-dimensional shapes and structure create patchwork that is far more interesting than most. You could incorporate this idea into your work.

HAVE PATIENCE

'Creating the finished product is a painstaking, long process,' Michael explains. 'I get two-thirds of the garment made up, then I hold up different swatches. I tried to scan in all the fabric swatches on to my computer, but it was a waste of time; it all looks completely different when it's made up.' And don't expect to love a mismatched piece first time, he advises. 'It's not something that you can go "Oh, that's right". You have to think about it, and come back to it later.'

INSIDER TRICKS

'When I piece two very different-coloured fabrics together, I match my thread colour to the darker one for the most invisible stitches.'

LAURA KEMSHALL, CONTEMPORARY PATCHWORK DESIGNER

lindakemshall.com

CASSANDRA ELLIS
ON PATCHWORKING WITH SCRAPS
THE QUILTS THAT TEXTILE DESIGNER CASSANDRA CREATES ARE DIVINE: CONTEMPORARY, YET CLASSIC, AND MOST CERTAINLY FUTURE HEIRLOOMS. *cassandraellis.co.uk*

BE IMAGINATIVE WITH YOUR FABRIC HUNT
'Start at home – yours, your parents' or grandparents'. There are always dresses or curtains or scraps of fabric that have great personal resonance. If you haven't bought textiles on your travels before, plan to pick some up on your next trip: it's a great way to incorporate special travel memories into something useful. Or try vintage clothing shops and charity shops.

IGNORE *SOME* OF THE RULES
'Traditional patchworkers are fairly adamant that only 100 per cent cotton in a quilting weight can be used. I don't believe this. I use a lot of silk, wool and different cottons in my quilts and they come out beautifully. However, do try to use similar weights of cloth: pairing a silk chiffon with a denim, for example, will not make a happy sewing experience and might mean harsher wear and tear.

DIFFICULT FABRICS CAN STILL BE USED
'Deal with anything particularly light (like lace) or difficult to work with (like a knit) by backing it with some cotton or bonding; lace will become stronger and knits won't stretch. Antique or vintage fabric might need a little more care and attention, too. Examine them carefully and discard any parts that are damaged, wearing out or stained.

STRAY AWAY FROM THE SQUARE
'You can "freestyle" quilts by sewing unusual or random-shaped pieces of fabric together, but you have to make sure your quilt ends up the shape you want. Watch that the patchwork doesn't start to curve or twist.'

'If you are joining two very small pieces together, use the back of your fingernail to press them flat, instead of ironing. They'll stay in place just long enough for you to sew them together.'

NICOLE MCCOOL, OWNER OF JUST SEW SEWING STUDIO

justsewbrighton.co.uk

'I always iron seams towards the darker fabric, so they don't show from the front.'

JANET GODDARD, QUILT DESIGNER

patchworkpatterns.co.uk

The project

THE PATCHWORK LOUIS CHAIR

You'll find many a lady lusting after a classic Louis chair. Alas, the ones for sale usually come with a three-figure price tag. Sure, this DIY version won't be as refined as one made by a pro upholsterer, but I'd bet no one we know could tell the difference.

HOW HARD IS IT TO DO?
The best part of two Saturdays (to allow the paint to dry between the weekends).

HOW LONG DOES IT TAKE?
It's certainly not the best project to start with, but put in the hours and anyone can do it.

MATERIALS

1 **A chair**

2 **Camera**

3 **Knife/staple lifter**

4 **Pliers**

5 **Sandpaper**

6 **Cleaning products**

7 **Primer** (FOR WOOD)

8 **Paint** (FOR WOOD)

9 **Paint brush**

10 **Upholstery fabric**

11 **Tailors' chalk**

12 **Fabric scissors**

13 **Needle**

14 **Strong thread**

15 **Pins**

16 **Staple gun** (AT LEAST 8MM STAPLES)

17 **Decorative stud strip** (ABOUT 4 METRES)

STEP 1
Find yourself a Louis chair. Try eBay, charity shops, Gumtree or Freecycle: you can usually pick one up from £25. Ignore the colour or finish, it's the shape you should focus on. Go for something with decent padding that springs back when you sit on it (although if it's terrible but the price tag is low, you could pay an upholsterer to replace this bit for you).

STEP 2
First, crack out your camera and take some close up photos of your chair. You will need to refer back to these later, so take as many as is necessary. Make notes too, if that helps.

STEP 3
Next, strip the chair of its fabric. You will have to remove some kind of decorative edging, either metal studding or fabric-covered cord first, so pull it off gently. The main pieces of fabric, on the seat and the back, will be held in place with staples or pins. Buy a special tool that helps lifts staples out, or insert a blunt butter knife behind the staple and twist and dislodge it. (Please be careful of your fingers.) Then, use pliers to pull the staples out completely. Keep taking photos throughout the process. Don't throw away the fabric you pull off – put it to one side to use as a template later.

STEP 4

At this point you'll be left with a wooden frame, with padding on the seat and potentially on the back too. (Or this back padding might just be sandwiched between fabric, and come off completely. However it comes off is the way you must put it back on.)

STEP 5

It's not necessary to remove the existing paint or varnish completely from the wood before repainting, however, it is vital that you prepare it properly. Use coarse sandpaper to rub down the wooden frame, then use warm soapy water to give it a good clean.

STEP 6

When the wood is dry, give it a coat of white primer. (Think of this like nail varnish – if you don't add a decent base, the beautiful colour you've painted will easily chip.) Stand your chair on a couple of layers of newspaper in a well-ventilated area. Pale wood will only need one coat; dark wood will probably need two or three.

STEP 7

Now add the main colour. I used a Plasti-kote fluorescent pink spray, so I covered the foam with scrap fabric before I started. Whether you use a spray or a brush-on paint from a tin, always check that it's suitable for wooden furniture, and always follow the instructions on the tin.

STEP 8

While the primer and paint dries, take to your sewing machine to prepare the new patchwork covers. Make the squares, triangles, or random shapes as small or as large as you like; the only rule is that the final covers need to be at least 2cm ($^3/_4$in) larger on all edges than the fabric you pulled off your chair in step 3. I expect you'll have four pieces of patchwork to make: one for the seat, one for the back, and two much smaller pieces to cover the padding on the arms.

STEP 9

Dig out those pieces of fabric you pulled off in step 3. Lay them on top of your patchwork, thinking carefully about the position. (Do you want the patchwork on the seat and back to line up, or at least be running in the same direction? Do you want it centred?) Draw around your template with tailor's chalk and add 2cm ($^3/_4$in) seams. Cut it out. Use your template to mark any cuts too (usually the seat piece has a few, so the fabric can be shaped around the arms).

STEP 10

Take your patchwork back to the machine and, 1cm ($^1/_2$in) from the line of chalk and do a line of very small stitches. This will prevent your patchwork from unravelling. Stitch around any snip you made too.

STEP 11

Once the paint is dry, you can start to re-cover your chair (I reckon this is always a two-person job). You must staple the new covers on in exactly the same way as they were before, so always refer to your photos and notes. Start with the back piece. Fold the extra 2cm ($^3/_4$in) seams under, giving the cover a nice neat edge (it makes the fabric stronger too). Have someone hold the cover in place while you staple. Don't staple around the cover clockwise: instead, think of it as a clock face. Staple at 12 first, then 6, 3 and 9, always pulling the fabric taut.

Follow with 1 and 11, 5 and 7, and so on. If the staples aren't flush to the wood, bang them in gently with a hammer. (If you put a staple in the wrong place, don't freak out. Remove it as you did in step 3. OK, you might chip the new paint job, but that can easily be retouched with a thin paintbrush later.)

STEP 12

Now do the two small arm pieces, again in exactly the same way as they came off (I stapled the sides first, then did the front and back). Remember to fold 2cm (^{3}/$_4$in) over on all edges before you staple.

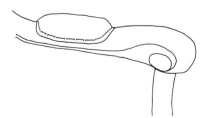

STEP 13

By now I reckon you have got this folding/pulling taut/stapling business mastered. Which is why I've left the trickiest part until now. Lay the seat cover in place. Start by folding/stapling the front. Then try the sides and the back. Do all the straight bits first, leaving the corners and arms until last.

STEP 14

If you've copied your template exactly, the slits you cut in the arms should fit nicely around them. Tuck the fabric under as much as is necessary. Finally, do the corners: this will involve folding the fabric as neatly as you can before tucking up the 2cm (^{3}/$_4$in) and stapling. This step is the most fiddly and might involve some trial and error, but don't give up – your chair is almost done.

It's time for tea. And a biscuit. Go on, you definitely deserve a biscuit.

STEP 15

Finishing off involves covering the join (where the fabric meets the wood), all the way around the chair. You can buy a thick, ready-made trim from a haberdashery and use superglue to stick that on, but I reckon metal studding gives a patchwork chair a bit of edge. Buy metal studding in strips, and simply hammer it in place. Always hammer in pins with lots of small knocks to the centre of the head, not with one heavy blow (otherwise they bend). Stand back, and admire your very, very hard work.

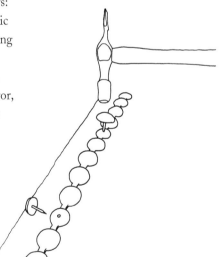

The extras

PATCHWORK YOURSELF A QUILT

It's the classic, most obvious project for patchwork, and the process is the same whatever sized quilt you make (it's just massively time consuming).

1. Create the top from patchwork (make it as simple or as intricate as you like).

2. Cut a piece of batting/wadding the same size (you can buy different thicknesses, depending on whether you're making a quilt for a baby, or want something that is machine washable).

3. Cut a piece of backing fabric which is also the same size (you might need to join a few pieces together to make it large enough).

4. Make a quilt 'sandwich': the backing goes right-side down, the batting gets laid on top, then add the patchwork, right-side up. Pin together.

5. Now to quilt! Hand sew running stitches or machine sew through all three layers, either along the edges of all the fabric pieces or randomly across the entire quilt. This binds the layers while also trapping air inside, which keeps you nice and toasty when in bed.

6. Get yourself some bias binding (strips of fabric with no raw edges) and sew it all around the edge of the quilt to finish it off.

PATCHWORK THE UNEXPECTED

Patchwork the bog-standard quilt and cushion cover and bag and, sure, it'll look great. But this technique really comes alive when it's used out of context to make something that isn't usually patchworked: a giant scarf, for instance. Pin two large rectangles of patchwork together, right sides facing, and backstitch around the edge, leaving a 10cm (4in) gap. Turn the scarf inside out, iron, and neatly oversew the gap closed.

Actually, patchwork can be used wherever you'd usually use one piece of fabric: to make a bow, a ruffle, a plush toy, a skirt, a fabric necklace, and much more. There is just one rule to follow: if you cut out a shape from a piece of patchwork (e.g. to make the front of a skirt), you must hem it, not leave it as a raw edge. That's because when you cut it out, you also cut through the thread that holds the pieces together. Wonderfully, when your new line of stitching crosses the old line of stitching, it keeps the thread securely in place.

KEEP IT SIMPLE

Patchwork doesn't have to be made up of different squares; you can keep it simple (which, to some people, means more stylish). The front of a cushion could be made with four large squares (why not use three squares of the same colour – white, perhaps – and a fourth highly patterned piece). The front of a purse could be made from two large rectangles patchworked together, to give a simple two-tone look. Or, patchwork three rectangles of varying widths and you get a striped effect.

PATCHWORK, WITHOUT THE FABRIC

I know, it sounds mad. But the gist of patchwork is that it's the same shape repeated again and again. And that in itself makes a rather lovely-looking pattern. So embrace the patchwork idea across your other crafts: découpage paper squares on to the top of a coffee table; carve out a triangle in a wooden block and print a patchworked pattern, or embroider a series of squares using satin stitch.

XXX stitch

Craft has a naughty side, and it's getting bigger and more explicit by the day. Welcome to a world where the stitching is erotic, the swearing is offensive and the craft is unlike anything you've seen before.

'I enjoy quilting the curves of the female body'

Among the traditional quilts in **Ferret** of Ferret Fabrication's collection you'll find a handful of impressive nudes, painstakingly created in patchwork *(ferfab.co.uk)*.

'At first I worked from photographs, but now I like to work with live models, just like an artist using oils might do. Getting the colours right is a satisfying challenge; I don't dye the fabrics myself to get the perfect shade, but work with off-the-shelf materials, often in blues, purples or reds, which I think have a more interesting feel than skin tones. I enjoy quilting the curves of the female body; their legs, their hair. I get asked why I don't do male nudes, but to be honest they are so untidy in certain places that I don't think I'd want to patchwork that.

'Some people called my first non-conventional quilt – Miss Baltimore – disgraceful and obscene. She was wearing a 1940s two-piece swimsuit, so I thought I'd be lynched when I exhibited my first nude. But I wasn't. Strangely, quilters don't seem to mind as long as you show the back view of people: they get far more worked up when there are breasts involved. Of course, there will always be factions who don't like my work – usually religious types who wouldn't take their children to an art gallery in case there were any pictures of naked people.

'But traditional quilters don't have a problem; although the images I patchwork are unusual, I use the same traditional techniques they use, and that wins me enough leeway.

'I fully expected the first nudes to be sold to a bachelor or art collector, but most have gone to older quilters – sixty-year-old ladies who hang them on their living-room wall. Some of these women clearly aren't as dead from the waist down as we like to think.'

'The first time I stitched "fuck" my heart raced a little'

Bee Franck mashes classic (meaning 'boring') cross-stitch patterns with everyone's favourite sarcastic, explicit and offensive phrases *(beefranck.tumblr.com)*.

'If you were to look at me, there's nothing that would suggest I do anything like this. I was actually raised Catholic and, to be honest, the first time I ever stitched 'fuck' my heart raced a little. I started cross stitching precisely to create these kinds of things, and it's probably the only reason I would have even taken it up. I like anything unexpected.

'I take antique patterns and rearrange them, so if you see it from a distance you'd think it was something old that Grandma could have stitched. Instead, it says something like "Nerds fuck harder". That's what makes it so fun to do. One of my favourite types of pattern to mess with is those old-fashioned, nasty ones that say something about a woman's place being in the home.'

'You won't find me stitching this stuff at work. Even if I do the non-offensive sections, someone will inevitably ask: "What's that going to say?", and I'm an awful liar. Someone had asked me to stitch "Stabby" for them and when I brought it into work I'd only finished the last four letters. A woman said: "That's nice, who's Abby?" I explained, and she just said "You're weird". I have to lie sometimes, though. Once, my parents were visiting and I thought it would be safe to work on the border and put the words in later. My dad, of course, asked what it would say and I just said "Oh, gee, I don't know yet". It was going to say "Hasty fellatio". My parents think it's really neat that there's so much interest in my work, but I'm not sure they quite get it.

'I don't hang my own pictures in my house, just things other people have made. They're just as explicit as my work, however. At the moment I sell things and I have the rest in a drawer upstairs. I guess I still have a little bit of the Catholic guilt, because I usually put them in there facing down.'

'Embroidering erotic scenes is more sentimental than drawing them'

Alaina Varrone is just as happy stitching pictures of alien abductions and Converse trainers as she is graphic scenes of erotic sex (yes, there are vaginas) *(flickr.com/photos/spiderspaw/)*.

'Like most art students I've always done life-drawing classes. Embroidering nudes was an economic decision at first; it's such an affordable craft. Then, during a really bad break-up, I found stitching erotic scenes was like a form of therapy. Creating some was like writing journal entries; others were about capturing the moments that I missed from my relationship and so desperately wanted to experience again.

'It's never been about shock value, or stitching sex and genitalia just for the sake of it. The pieces discuss and express a certain kind of sexuality. Embroidering these scenes seems more sentimental than if I were to draw or photograph them and I think the thought and emotion that goes into creating them really comes through. They have touched a nerve with the feminist movement, and many young girls get in touch saying they really identify with the images or that I've inspired them to experiment with the medium of embroidery to express themselves, too. They're the best reactions. The worst come from people who hold really old-fashioned stereotypes about embroidery and have nothing to say about them except: "Ooh, Grandma's getting frisky".

'Each erotic piece can take months to create. It's important to me that each stitch is done just right, because I feel like people give my work more respect and take me more seriously when it is technically impressive, too. So much effort and emotion goes into them that I don't know how to quantify how much they should sell for. And I haven't sold any yet, because I don't think I'm ready to part with them.'

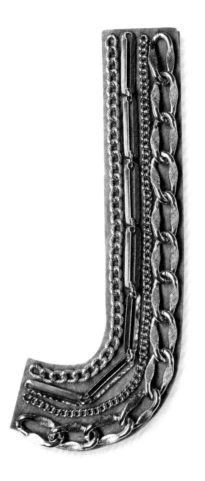

Jewellery making

From cuffs to cocktail rings, anything is possible when you've got the hang of this jewellery-making malarkey. You'll never be without the perfect accessories again, whether you like to rock a statement necklace, or prefer your jewels dainty and elegant.

The technique

MATERIALS

1 Findings

These are the nuts and bolts that make up a piece of jewellery. What you need depends on what you're making. There are clasps to fasten necklaces and bracelets (you can get all sorts: lobster catches, bolt rings, box snaps, toggles and more), bases for earrings (plain hoops, studs, hook wires for dangly ones), backs for brooches, bases for cufflinks and so on. The most useful? The humble jump ring – a circle of metal wire used to connect objects to other objects.

2 A base

Traditionally a chain or beading wire, but you can use anything – pretty ribbon, strips of leather or fabric ... so long as it's thin and necklace-y.

3 Decorations

Beads, charms, pendants, or anything with a hole in. Actually, as long as you can make a hole in it somehow, you can use it to embellish your jewellery.

4 Pliers

Get round-nosed or needle-nosed pliers for bending wire and findings, and jewellery pliers for cutting it.

5 Wire

It's useful to have some knocking around to create pendants or giant jump rings. Buy cheap stuff (say, 99p for three metres) or 24ct gold (which is very pricey).

GETTING STARTED

Buy specialist materials from beading shops, or just throw together bits and bobs from around your flat. No matter what you use, there are a handful of ways to put it together.

THE TRADITIONAL METHOD

This is the most well-known technique for making necklaces, bracelets and earrings. Your chain or pre-bought earring hook is the base, and you add beads, pendants, charms and more.

FIX IT

The secret is knowing what to do with a jump ring. Open it using round-nosed pliers, slip the two things on that you want to join together, then use the pliers to close it again. Simple.

No matter what type of clasp you use, 99 per cent of the time you'll use this method to fix it to the end of a chain.

Pendants are attached this way too, to chains or to earring hooks. (Your jump ring isn't big enough? Cut a piece of wire, wrap it around a pencil or similar, and use the round-nosed pliers to help you make your own.)

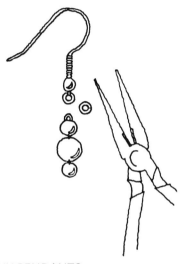

DIY PENDANTS

As long as it has a hole, you can fix anything to a chain. Thread it on to a head pin (a little piece of pre-cut wire with a flat bottom), then use round-nosed pliers to bend the top around into a loop, slip this through a jump ring and it's ready to be attached.

If your object has too big a hole (or you want a multi-bead charm), thread a smaller bead on first so the larger one can't slip. Alternatively, cut a length of wire, bend a loop at one end, thread on your beads, then make another loop at the top.

With this method you have the added bonus of being able to fix either end to a chain or earring hook.

THREAD IT

A nice-and-simple method for making necklaces and bracelets. Choose a base – chain, ribbon, beading wire, even lengths of rope, knitted I-cord or strips of fabric – and thread on your objects. So long as the objects (beads, pendants, etc.) have a hole big enough, your base can be as chunky as you want.

Before you cut a length, check in the mirror that it'll be long enough, then add on a few centimetres to either end to allow room for tying.

There are no rules. Thread on one statement bead or cover the entire base with beads (just remember to leave enough unthreaded so you can tie it up). And don't just stick to beads; anything with a hole can work. I've seen safety pins, ring pulls, even stationery threaded on to a necklace (though just because you can, it doesn't mean you should). Anything that will look better positioned flat to the chest should be attached to a jump ring first (as below), then you just thread on the jump ring.

Between every bead, tie a knot in your base, then, should it fall off your neck or wrist, the beads won't come off and get lost. (Or, if you use a chain for your base, the clasp should be bigger than the last items to be threaded.)

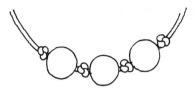

FINISHING OFF
If you've used a chain, add a clasp to either end to secure. If you've used ribbon, fabric or thin leather, tie a bow (which can then easily be undone) or buy special clasps that you slip the material into and squash down using round-nosed pliers. (My advice? Put a blob of glue inside them first.)

FABRIC JEWELLERY

Fabric? Jewellery? Really? Yes, indeed. Though not the typical material of choice, it's a brilliant way to create something unique.

THE FABRIC NECKLACE

Cut a bib shape from paper and check it sits nicely on your chest. Draw around it on a piece of felt, but don't cut it out just yet. Instead, decorate inside the lines with stitches (page 28), sequins or gems (page 68), appliqué (page 212) or fabric embellishments (page 116). (Although you're not meant to put felt in an embroidery hoop, because it stretches, you can just this once, as long as the entire bib shape fits inside the hoop.) Be sure to leave a couple of millimetres uncovered around each edge.

When you're done, carefully cut out your felt shape and sew a piece of ribbon to the back of each side. Cut a second piece of felt to exactly the same size and, using a backstitch or oversew stitch, sew it to the back of the decorated piece to hide the messy stitching.

Bracelets can be made in a similar fashion. Rather than a bib shape, cut a rectangle of felt just long enough to go around your wrist, and sew ribbon (or hook and eyes or press studs) to each short end for tying.

ALTERNATIVELY...
Should you want to add anything made of fabric to a chain, set of beads, or similar, just sew them on using strong general-purpose thread. But keep it neat: your stitches won't always stay hidden.

RINGS, CUFFLINKS, STUD EARRINGS AND BROOCHES

With the right base and a blob of glue or a few stitches, these pieces of jewellery are easy peasy to make. Using the information on glue on page 68, fix stones, gems, buttons or whatever on to the flat surfaces of your ring, cufflinks or stud-earring base.

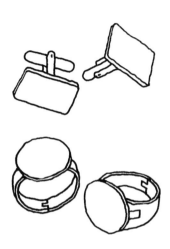

Brooches can be made in the same way but have the added bonus that they can be sewn on to fabric embellishments too.

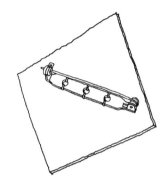

COMMON PROBLEMS

There's no way I can make a hole in this object. So you want to hang it off a necklace, but drilling a hole isn't possible. That's OK. Try tying wrapping wire around it, creating a little cage that it can sit in, then slip this on to a jump ring. You might make a feature of the wire, or keep it simple so that everyone's eye is on the amazing bead/gem/thing you simply had to have on a necklace.

My wire keeps snapping. Bend it too often in the same place and the wire will weaken and eventually snap. When making a loop in the top of a head pin, for example, if you don't get it right by the tenth attempt, consider starting again with another pin.

The masterclass

TATTY DEVINE

ON CREATING JEWELLERY FROM JUNK

ROSIE WOLFENDEN AND HARRIET VINE, FOUNDERS OF THIS CULT JEWELLERY BRAND, AND AUTHORS OF *HOW TO MAKE JEWELLERY WITH TATTY DEVINE*, KNOW EXACTLY HOW TO MAKE SOMETHING FROM NOTHING; THEIR FIRST PRODUCTS WERE MADE FROM SCRAP LEATHER FOUND IN A BAG ON THE STREET. *tattydevine.com*

ALWAYS BE A MAGPIE

'Whether you look in charity shops, car boot sales or jumble sales, dig through the little boxes full of bits and bobs. Use coins, cracker toys, cake decorations or old sewing tools to embellish jewellery.

TURN THE ORDINARY INTO THE EXTRAORDINARY

'Items that seem uninteresting on their own can have massive impact when displayed en masse. Think heads of old zips, cracker toys, marbles or pencil stubs.

THINK ABOUT HOLES

'Look for trinkets and sundries with holes in already, like key rings or horse brasses. Or, if you have access to a drill, you can make your own holes in anything made from wood, plastic and soft metal. Make friends with the local DIY shop and they will to help you choose the right drill bit for the job.

GET TO KNOW FINDINGS

'Bead shops are full of weird findings that you can stick to strange objects to make them into jewellery. Or, raid DIY shops for larger eyelets and split rings that aren't stocked by normal jewellery suppliers.

SPIT AND POLISH

'Remove all traces of grease if you want to give glue the best chance of sticking; it's a real bore to lose your snazzy new brooch when the brooch back hasn't stuck properly. Clean your old junk well, but be careful not to remove the lustre of age.'

INSIDER TRICKS

'To make your jewellery extra special, look for interesting clasps and use a jump ring to add a tiny charm to it.'

SINEAD KOEHLER, JEWELLERY DESIGNER AND FOUNDER OF BRIXTON'S CRAFTY FOX MARKET

galavant.etsy.com

LARA BOHINC

ON MAKING A STANDOUT PIECE OF JEWELLERY
THE JEWELLERY DESIGNER HAS WORKED FOR GUCCI
AND LANVIN, AND NOW HER OWN LABEL IS COVETED BY
THE LIKES OF KATE MOSS, CHERYL COLE AND MICHELLE
OBAMA. *larabohinc.com*

BE CAREFUL WITH COLOUR

'It's a question of wearability,' she believes. 'If you've got something with lots of green stones, there are so many things you can't wear it with.' Lara prefers to use gold, silver, white and diamonds, so no matter what colour you wear, your jewellery won't clash. Create interest by mixing up shapes or textures, rather than colour.

EVEN SIMPLE PIECES NEED CAREFUL PLANNING

'The problem with some small jewellery is that it doesn't get the creative merit that it deserves.' No matter how small or simple, you can still make a statement if you pay attention to every last detail, she believes: the colour, texture and shape of any material you use.

DISOBEY THE RULES

Should you mix gold and silver, or keep to classic shapes? Rules are too constricting, Lara argues. 'In the old days it used to be that bags and shoes had to match, now there's no one who would dream of doing that, it would look outdated.'

GO LARGE, OR VERY SMALL

'People are always more interested in size,' she says. 'Scale is something that people appreciate. They think about it more and they remember it more.' Don't play safe with something of average size: statement pieces are either minute (meaning delicate and fine) or oversized (chunky, thick and large).

LOOK FURTHER FOR INSPIRATION

'I've based jewellery on mathematical models and buildings,' says Lara. 'Or I can start with a very simple thing … a circle, a texture or a mood.'

MAKE IT FEEL GOOD TO WEAR

'Some pieces look beautiful, but when you pick them up you don't want to wear it because it's too clunky or too heavy,' she says. 'It has to feel sensual.'

'You don't need to be a silversmith to make impressive silver jewellery these days. Use precious-metal clay, an amazing, eco-friendly material that you shape by hand. Once made, burn away the clay with a blowtorch, and it leaves nothing but 99.9 per cent pure silver.'

AMITY ROACH IS ETSY'S UK COMMUNITY MANAGER AND A JEWELLERY DESIGNER

etsy.com/people/AmityUK

The project

A DOUBLE-CHAIN NECKLACE

Whether you like your jewellery to make a statement or simply blend in with your outfit, tailor this basic design to however you like it.

HOW LONG DOES IT TAKE?
It's pretty simple.

HOW HARD IS IT TO DO?
You'll have it done by the time the Sunday afternoon film finishes.

MATERIALS

1   Chain

2   Jump rings

3   Clasp

4   Round-nosed pliers

5   Wire cutters

6   Wire

7   A selection of beads

STEP 1
Your first job? To make a basic necklace. Cut two lengths of chain, one shorter than the other (mine were 60cm/24in and 72cm/28in). Slip one end of both chains on to a jump ring, and close it. Slip the other ends of the chains on to a second jump ring, and close that too. Add a clasp to these jump rings to finish.

STEP 2
Now to make a few beaded pendants (follow the instructions on page 181 for how to make a DIY pendant with loops at both ends). My necklace had three – two on one chain, one on the other – and I used gold, clear and pearl-coloured beads of varying sizes. Add as many or as few as you like, mixing up colours, sizes and textures of beads to your taste.

Add a jump ring to each looped end of your beaded pendants.

STEP 3
To work out where the beaded pendants are best positioned, lay the basic necklace out on a flat surface. Play around with them, placing the pendants on top of the chains to get an idea of what they'll look like. Do you want them all up one side, all at the bottom, or all on one chain? Take a quick snap on your phone before you move them about, so you can compare ideas more easily.

STEP 4
Are you happy with where they're placed? Excellent. Cut a chunk of chain the length of the beaded pendant using wire cutters. Replace this chunk with a beaded pendant, using the jump rings you attached in step 3. Repeat for the other beads.

STEP 5
Because it's the details that make jewellery so special, I added a small charm to the necklace clasp. To do this, slip a bead on to a head pin, make a loop in the top with round-nosed pliers. Use a jump ring to attach it to a short length of chain, then to another to attach it to one of the jump rings you added in step 1.

ALTERNATIVELY ...
A two-chain bracelet is made in almost the same way; the only differences are that the beaded pendants tend to be shorter (what with wrists being so much smaller than necks) and the chains are the same length.

The extras

THE ALTERNATIVE CHARM BRACELET

There might be plenty of ready-made charms to buy from bead shops, but nothing says I-put-some-thought-into-making-this like a bracelet with handmade charms. Scout around the house for those spare, little mementos you have: a bead that fell off a favourite bag, a shell from a beach you have fond memories of, the earring you wore to your school prom. Find a way of attaching these items to a jump ring, then slip those jump rings on to a bracelet-sized length of chain or cord. Add them at even intervals all the way around the bracelet, or attach just two or three in the same place (especially if you're not a statement jewellery kind of person).

FEELING WIRED

Once you can open a jump ring, you're well on your way to learning the basics of bending wire. Using your fingers and a pair of round-nosed pliers, you can turn any length of wire into something far more interesting. Start with a basic shape – a diamond or a heart – and use these as pendants (I like to slip a few on to a pretty ribbon and tie them around my wrist). Once you've got a feel for it, try bending your initial, or even your name. Write it on a piece of paper in clear, simple, joined-up writing and use this as your guide. (Yes, it's just like a folksy version of *Sex and the City*'s Carrie necklace.)

You needn't limit yourself to using this technique to make jewellery, either. Wire shapes can be used to decorate birthday cards (glue or stitch them on to the front), napkin rings, picture frames, lampshades and much more. If you can get your hands on thick, sculptural wire from an art shop, you can use the same principle to bend giant shapes to hang from picture hooks (think words like 'hello' or a handful of stars).

LOOK AT THE ROCK ON THAT!

The bigger the better, right? The easiest way to make a beast of a cocktail ring is to buy a base and simply glue a large gem, button, pendant or stone to the front. Or, buy a ring base with a huge front and stick lots of smaller gems and sequins and beads to it. Alternatively, you could splash out on a fancy ring base that has a loop or two sticking out of the front (it'll be – ooh – 40p more) and whip up a cluster ring. Make a handful of mini pendants, attach each to a jump ring and slip each jump ring through the loop.

BEJEWEL YOUR BAG

It's those well-thought-out details than make an object really special. To top off a plain clutch or purse, make a small, matching pendant: slip the end through a jump ring and slip the jump ring through the pull of a zip. Should you want something more lavish (and practical) for your clutch, add a wrist strap. Cut a length of chain/cord/ribbon long enough to slide around your wrist easily, and decorate it with beads, pendants and other pretty things.

If you've used a chain, attach each end to a single split ring, then slip this through the pull of a zip (a slip ring is that part of a key ring that all the other keys are slipped on to). If you've used something like a ribbon, poke one end through the zip and tie the ends together in a secure knot.

If your bag has its straps attached to the main body with split rings, these can be restyled using this technique too. Cut off the old strap and replace it with a big, chunky chain of the same length (I use a cheap chain belt from the high street instead of buying chains from a specialist jewellery shop).

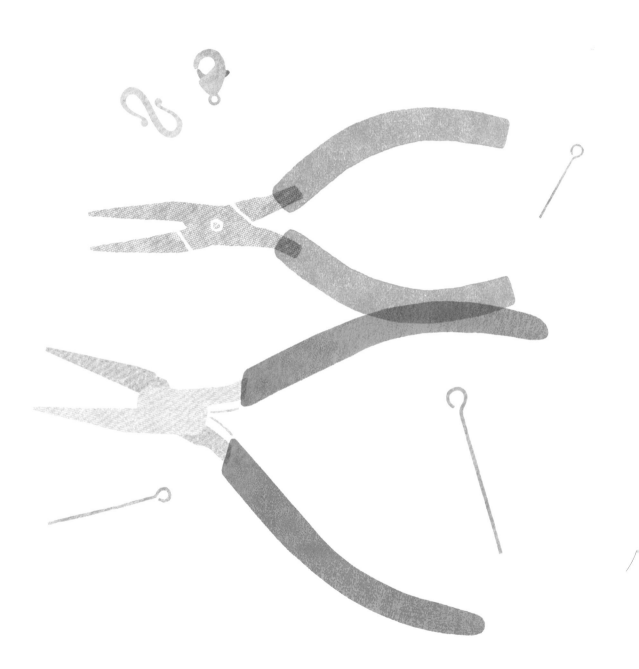

Craft legends

The following five people are some of the biggest names in the craft world today. They're our inspiration, the ones we look to when we're staring at a blank canvas and have no idea what to do with it. But if they're the greats, then who on earth do they look up to when they're feeling uncreative? I asked, and they revealed …

Kaffe Fassett on … Duncan Grant and Vanessa Bell

For four decades Kaffe Fassett has reigned supreme over the world of textiles, creating the most sought-after quilts, mosaics and knits (kaffefassett.com).

'Charleston House is an extraordinary place and one I am very much inspired by. It was created by the artists Duncan Grant and Vanessa Bell as a country retreat for London's Bloomsbury Group in the early nineteenth century; the likes of Virginia Woolf stayed there. The pair turned it into their personal fantasy palace; they made rag rugs, painted their own wallpaper, and in doing so created a place of great beauty.

'I'm in the process of doing what they did. I paint murals and do needlepoints and make my own wallpaper. We have a mosaic around our fireplace made of shards I picked up on my walks around Hampstead Heath. I love the idea of turning the things in our everyday lives – like a chair seat or a cushion – into something beautiful and intriguing that we want to look at and look at again.'

Emily Peacock on … Jean Lurçat

Emily revolutionised the world of needlepoint with her colourful, contemporary tapestry kits; it's never been quite the same (or as quaint and crusty) since (*emilypeacock.com*).

'I discovered Jean Lurçat, the French tapestry designer, at a time when I was living in France and searching for what to do next. I knew I wanted to design needlework, but I was stuck about what to do. On entering his atelier near St Céré, I saw the incredible designs he had created; scorching suns, fish thirsting for water, the bright stars I would see on a clear night over the Pyrenées. As well as being a creative, he was also a left-wing political activist – his tapestries incorporate poetic lines that reflect his views. So much of this man, his environment and his passions are woven into his work.

'What I find so inspiring about him is not only his ability to breathe new life into a traditional craft, but also that you can find inspiration from where you stand. There is a lot of merit in upholding tradition, but craft can become stuck and repetitive. Jean Lurçat set me on a path to open my eyes, find my own voice and live from the inside out.'

Rachael Matthews on … Beatrix Potter

You can hold Rachael responsible for the modern craft craze; it all started back in 2003 when her knitting group, Cast Off, hit the headlines for knitting in pubs. She now runs the Prick Your Finger knitting shop (*prickyourfinger.com*).

'I love so many craft people, but the person who is most important to me is Beatrix Potter. While she lived in the Lake District – the place I grew up in – she spun all her yarn and wove and painted the landscape around her. I have one of her spinning wheels; it's not one I ever use (you have to strap your foot to the pedal to get it to work), but it's this fantasy object that I find really inspiring.

'As I get older, Beatrix Potter becomes more poignant, and I get more inspired by her values and bravery. She published books even though her parents didn't want her to, she stayed unmarried, she ran away to the Lake District to live a sustainable life, farming, spinning and painting. She stuck to her guns and puts an awful lot of love into very simple things.'

Amy Butler on ... Kaffe Fassett

Every haberdashery I've been into in the last five years has stocked this designer's fabric. No wonder she's so in demand; the patterns and colours she uses are simply stunning (*amybutlerdesign.com*).

'Kaffe never plays it safe. He will never shy away from a confident colour combination, or sacrifice his vision for anything. It's so inspiring for me to see a peer create so bravely, and I think any crafter would do well to take a leaf from his book in that respect. He has a rare eye for colour; truly, I have never seen another artist who works with colour the way he does. His quilts, needlepoints, fabrics and knits are like exquisite works of art and nothing makes my mouth water more.

'He works from such a personal place, and to witness the level of heart in what he does is moving and empowering. He puts a great deal of passion into absolutely everything he does and you can feel it in his work. We're lucky to have such a gifted art legend in our lives.'

Dawn Bibby on ... William Morris

The former QVC presenter is probably the craft world's biggest celebrity. Her scrapbooking and paper craft designs have garnered her a legion of dedicated followers who lap up her TV shows, blog posts, products and much more. (*dawnbibbycrafting.blogspot.com* or *topazcrafts.tv*)

'My father was an antiques dealer, so as a young girl I was surrounded by antique fabrics and furniture. I loved the ornate, textured patterns that William Morris, the Arts and Crafts textile designer working in the late nineteenth century, is renowned for. At college I studied textiles and fashion – and went on to design knitwear and later on ranges of craft materials – but William Morris has always influenced me. I used to go through all his books and use them as inspiration in my artwork.

'I use lots of flourishes and flower heads, as he did. But I have translated those elements differently – my designs are less traditional, and more pretty. I try to do what he was so great at: making very intricate patterns look sensational. I'm a bit of a magpie, so I love my work to be made up of lots of metallics, sparkles, glitter, and plenty of detailing.'

'TRANSFORM YOUR WARDROBE'

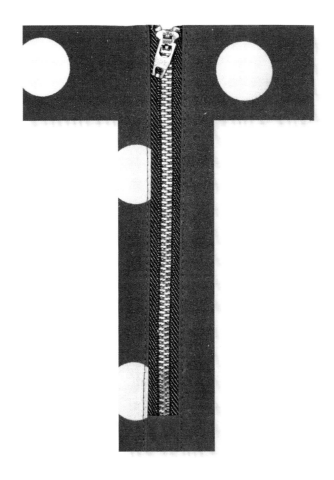

Tailoring

The perfect dress doesn't exist in a shop. It's the wrong colour, or slightly too big or slightly too small. It's too plain, or the fancy one doesn't fit your perfect budget. Learn to alter and customise clothes, however, and your wardrobe will become much more exciting place.

The technique

MATERIALS

1 **Medium-sized needle**

2 **Multi-purpose thread**
   Always match the colour of the thread to the colour of the garment.

3 **Pins**

4 **Fabric scissors**

5 **Tape measure/ruler**

6 **Tailor's chalk**

7 **Stitch ripper**
   The most effective way to unpick seams.

8 **Newspaper and pencil**
   For making templates.

THE ALTERATIONS ACADEMY

MAKE IT FITTED

The baggy blouse, T-shirt or dress that you never wear can easily be turned into something more tailored and more flattering. (So long as it doesn't have a side zip. If it does, this won't work.)

Turn your garment inside out and put it on. (You'll need a hand for this next part, or stand in front of a mirror). Pin all the way up both sides where you want the new seam to be.

This line needn't follow the original stitching, but you must take in an equal amount on both sides, otherwise the garment will look wonky. Walk around, sit down and jump around to make sure the new fit is comfortable. Readjust the pins if necessary, then take it off.

To create the new seam, sew a backstitch along the line of the pins (when doing this on a machine, I tack first, remove the pins, then do the final stitches). For extra security, do another line of stitches 1mm away from the first. If you're sure you never want to wear it baggy again, cut off the excess fabric, 1cm away from your newly stitched seam.

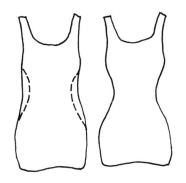

ALTERNATIVELY ...

Should you need to make your favourite shirt a little larger, that's possible, too, as long as it has seams bigger than 2cm ($^3/_4$in) (see page 21 for a seams masterclass). Unpick the side stitching, then stitch back together as above, but with a smaller seam.

MAKE IT SHORTER

Turn midi-skirts into minis, or give full-length trousers a chic crop, because sometimes it's the shape, not the style or colour, that you're bored with.

Unpick the existing seam carefully and put on your garment. (If you want to chop loads off the bottom – say, turn jeans into denim shorts – don't bother about careful unpicking.) Have a friend (or do it in the mirror) mark where you want the new length to be, either with tailor's chalk or a pin.

Take off the garment and measure the distance between the bottom of the fabric and the mark; use this measurement to mark a line the whole way around the garment. It's important that the distance between the line and the bottom of the garment is exactly the same all the way around, and on both legs if it's trousers. (Are you making something more than 3cm ($1^1/_4$in) shorter? First, cut most of the excess fabric off, leaving it just 3cm longer than you want it to be.)

Now turn your garment inside out. Fold the bottom edge up so that the fold line is where the marked line is. Give it a good iron or pin it in place, then try it on again to check the new length. It's OK? Excellent. Time to hand sew.

Poke the needle into the hem (see top right) about 2mm below the top edge (but don't go into the outer fabric yet). Then, poke the needle into the outer fabric just above the hemline, just to the left. Make a tiny stitch in the outer fabric – no more than 1mm – then poke the needle back through the hem. Your two diagonal stitches should look like an upside-down 'V'. Repeat this stitch all the way around the hem, checking the front of the garment occasionally to ensure the stitches are so small that they can barely be seen.

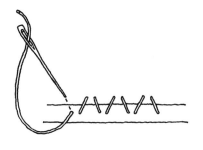

ALTERNATIVELY …

✂ *There is a no-sew option* (but I don't condone it as it's not as sturdy as sewing. I'm just telling you to be nice). Mark and fold as above, but instead of sewing it together, cut a length of fusible webbing, tuck it between the two layers of fabric and iron in place (see page 20).

✂ *You can also make something longer,* but only ever by a few centimetres. Turn the garment inside out and look at the hem. How much is there? If it's more than 2cm, great. If it's not, sorry, no can do. Unpick the existing seam, give it a very, very good iron to get rid of that crease, then follow the instructions above to make a new hem (try to keep a 1cm seam where possible).

MAKE IT SLEEVELESS

Snip the sleeves off, about 2cm (³/₄in) from the armhole. Tuck this excess into the armhole and, very neatly, stitch it in place, like a hem. Or, if there's stitching there already (as on a fitted shirt), use a backstitch and sew over these existing stitches.

ALTERNATIVELY …

Long sleeves can be made into short sleeves using the 'make it shorter' tutorial above. But you needn't hem it, as above: you can do a neat backstitch (or straight stitch on a machine). Be sure to start sewing on the underside of the sleeve, and keep the beginning and end as neat as possible (if hand sewing, stitch those securing stitches into the excess fabric of the seam).

THE REWORKING CLASS

Take something plain, old or unworn, and make it better. Here's how …

EMBELLISH IT

Whoa! You don't need any more on this. There's a whole chapter on encrusting on page 68, and one on embellishments on page 116, and one on macramé on page 156.

There I show you how to add trims, edging, ribbon, bows, clusters and more. Flick back and adapt for your clothes (I like mini bows on cuffs and socks and fabric clusters around a neckline of a top).

Just remember that loads of messy stitches at the back of clothing can rub against your skin, so keep it as neat as possible. If you've

got something über-stretchy, tack a piece of stabiliser on the back before you stitch (see page 18).

ALL ZIPPED UP

These days you'll pay a shedload more for a dress that has a stand-out coloured or black zip in the back instead of something that matches. But replacing a zip really isn't that hard.

Take a photo of the zip first, for reference. Using a seam ripper (or sewing scissors) unpick it – be careful you don't snip the garment, and get rid of any scraggly threads. Measure the zip, then buy a replacement. Ideally your new zip will be the same length, but if it's not, never mind: buy one that's longer, zip it up and chop it to size with strong scissors. (If it's a metal zip you'll need to do it a little differently.)

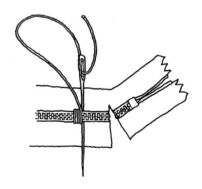

Cut the tape each side of the teeth, then twist the teeth back and forth at this point to break). Then, sew loads of stitches across the teeth where the metal catch was on your old zip and your new zip is ready.

Pin it in place in one of two ways:

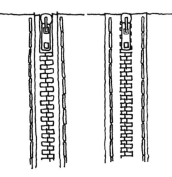

✄ *Position it in exactly the same place* as the old zip was (referring back to the photo), so most of the zip tape is inside the garment.

✄ *Pin it on top* of the fabric, so all the zip tape is exposed and on the outside of the garment.

Now, hand sew it in place using a backstitch (I think it's too fiddly to do on a machine but if you've got time, go for it). Check your photo: the stitching should follow the same line as before, no matter how you pinned it in.

ALTERNATIVELY …
Even if there isn't a functioning zip on your garment, it doesn't mean you can't make it look like there's one (a long one running all the way down the back of a dress or white shirt looks great). Simply pin it in place and sew it on; no one need know it's not real.

ADDING A PANEL
A naff print on the front of a T-shirt could be cut out and replaced with a similar colour, but different-textured fabric. A panel of lace could be sewn into the low-V of a top. The yoke of a shirt could be unpicked and replaced with a contrasting colour of fabric. Or, chop out panels randomly. (One thing to remember: if you've got a stretchy top and you add a large panel of non-stretchy fabric, it won't stretch as much any more.)

There are a few ways to add a panel, depending on how tidy you want it to look.

✄ *The it's-already-got-a-cut-out method.* Some garments have feature holes already cut or low necklines you want to fill up. If so, cut a piece of fabric large enough to cover the hole, turn your garment inside out and pin it in place. Turn it the right way around, and backstitch around the edge of the hole, through both layers of fabric.

✄ *The easy-but-rough method.* Cut out your panel using fabric scissors; you're not doing anything to these freshly cut edges, so expect them to fray a bit (that's the 'rough' part of the title). Lay this cut-out piece on top of the replacement panel fabric and draw around it, adding 1cm (1/2in) seams. Cut it out. Turn your garment inside out, and pin your new panel in place. Turn it the right way around, and check it looks OK. Happy? Good. Backstitch it on.

✄ *The neat-but-not-so-easy method.* Using tailor's chalk, draw on your panel. Cut it out, but not along the line; 2cm (³/₄in) away from it, inside the panel. Now's the time to brush up on the seams class on page 21, because the extra 2cm of fabric left will be your seam. Fold this inside your garment, snipping curves and corners as necessary, making a neat edge where the line of chalk is. Pin or iron these seams in place. Finally, cut a new panel 2cm bigger that the hole, pin it inside the garment, and attach using a backstitch.

ALTERNATIVELY...

If your panel isn't see-through (think lace or mesh) you needn't do any of this cutting out malarkey; instead turn to page 212 and use the invisible appliqué technique to stitch on a panel.

ADDING A COLLAR

Dresses and T-shirts look ever so pretty with a little collar added: either make your own or steal one from another garment (keep your eye out for cheap tops with interesting collars in sales or charity shops).

✄ *The I-nicked-it method.*
Ideally, the collar should be from a neck about the same size as the neckline of your garment (if it's bigger, trim it, if it's smaller, you'll have to make a feature of the gap, or hide it at the back). Carefully unpick your new collar with a seam ripper or sewing scissors (or cut it off, with an extra 1cm of fabric attached). Pin on to your new top, so the rough edges are inside the garment and sew it on using a back- or oversew stitch, whichever is most appropriate.

✄ *The I-made-it-myself method.*
Peter Pan collars are the most simple to construct from scratch.

Measure the diameter of your garment's neck, and use this to make two templates, as below.

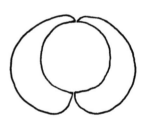

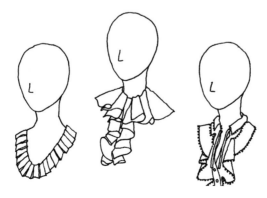

✂ *Add 1cm* all the way around each template, and cut out two pieces from each. Pin the two pieces together, right side facing, and backstitch around, 1cm from the edge. Leave 3cm (1in) unstitched in a not-very-visible place. Use this hole to turn the pieces the right way around and then iron flat. Oversew the hole closed. Repeat for the other two pieces, and stitch in place around the neckline of your garment. Doesn't it look fancy?

ALTERNATIVELY ...

Mix up the I-made-it-myself method by making a larger or different-shaped collar: the basic premise always stays the same.

COMMON PROBLEMS

My seams and hems always break. Have you secured the stitches well enough? Take a look at page 17 and check you're starting and finishing off a line of sewing properly. Otherwise, upgrade to extra-strength thread, invest in a sewing machine or dance around a little less.

My customised clothes always look 'homemade'. If things look a little too *Blue Peter* for your liking, pay close attention to the next two pages.

The masterclass

TOPSHOP

ON THE RULES OF REWORKING CLOTHES

MELANIE ROWSON IS DESIGN MANAGER AT TOPSHOP.

topshop.com

THE RIGHT TRIM CAN WORK WONDERS

'You can find some great lace trims or appliqué lace in haberdasheries that you could sew down the edge of a shirt.' Or, if you want something harder, she suggests leather and studs. 'Add panels or patches of leather trim for a fetish look. Studding florals always looks great because they take on a harder edge.' (To add a stud, pierce the fabric with the stud's prongs, then use the back of a knife to fold the prongs down and secure). 'If you've got a bright silver stud, an antiquing solution will make it look old and tarnished.'

LEARN TO TAILOR YOUR VINTAGE

'The evolvement of modern vintage is defined by new shapes and not rehashing old silhouettes literally. It's about doing something different to it to make it look up to date,' she says. 'Update vintage dresses by cutting off their sleeves or making them shorter. Or take the shoulder pads out of an 1980s top.'

TURN OUTERWEAR INTO A MODERN CLASSIC

'Use vintage fur – not cheap, nasty fur – to embellish outerwear. You might stitch an amazing vintage fur stole to the hood of a parka to turn it into something quite modern, or take a little tweed jacket and add fur to the collar.' Your garment should be heavy enough to take the weight of the fur.

EMBRACE HYBRID GARMENTS

'Take three garments to bits and mix them all up so you have a different-coloured front, a different-coloured back and a different-coloured sleeve,' she explains. 'Carefully unpick the garments at the seams, then re-sew carefully and as neatly as possible.'

THE NEW DYEING

'This isn't about dyeing something to change the colour of it. It's over-dyeing a bright floral print with a grey, so you still get a faint hint of the pattern, for example. It can be done with check or any pattern that's too garish.'

INSIDER TRICKS

ELLE
ON CUSTOMISING WITH FLAIR
NATALIE WANSBROUGH-JONES IS *ELLE*'S SENIOR FASHION EDITOR. *elleuk.com*

BE TRUE TO YOURSELF

'What works depends on the person wearing it; there's no hard-and-fast rule. Fashion should be fun, creative and about individuality.' But, she warns, 'You need to understand what suits your body shape, what colours suit you and what you can and cannot wear.' It's no good covering a dress with pink sequins if a) you never wear pink, or b) you never wear sequins.

STICK TO THE RULES OF SHOPPING

Take your head out of the craft box and think about materials as you would think about buying clothes. 'I have made fashion mistakes because I buy colours that don't suit me, because something is on sale, or I think it's a bargain,' she says. 'I end up not wearing it and getting rid of it.' Whenever you customise or rework, 'Stick to your own sense of style and to the kind of woman you are', she advises. You might love polka-dot fabric, but if you would never wear spots, save it for another project.

LOOK TO THE CATWALK

'We have an intern who always does things that shouldn't necessarily work, like safety-pinning parts of her skirt or her T-shirt, but it always looks fantastic. She's looking at the designers and slightly mimicking what they do: the cut of their clothes, the pattern, the way they drape.'

'Try not to focus critically on the details of your work. Nobody else will notice wonky stitching or slight sizing imbalances. Over time, you will stand back and see your creation as a whole, forgetting about these flaws.'

ROSIE MARTIN, DIY COUTURE

diy-couture.co.uk

'Always steam-iron your fabric before cutting: you want it to do any shrinking before you cut it. Silk crepe and linen are the worst at shrinking – beware!'

LISA COMFORT, FOUNDER OF SEW OVER IT SEWING STUDIO

sewoverit.co.uk

The project

THE T-SHIRT DRESS

Rather than faff about making a dress from scratch, this project gives you licence to create a classic-shaped garment in any colour, style or shape you like. Sweet, huh?

HOW HARD IS IT TO DO?
It's not child's stuff, but take it slowly and I reckon even a beginner can do a good job.

HOW LONG DOES IT TAKE?
Swap a day's shopping for a day of this (at least you can be sure you'll have a great dress at the end of it).

MATERIALS

1 **Scrap fabric**

2 **Tailor's chalk**

3 **Scissors**

4 **Ruler/tape measure**

5 **Fabric** (SHIRTING COTTON OR THICKER)

6 **Pins**

7 **Needle**

8 **Thread**

9 **T-shirt**

10 **Shirring elastic**

STEP 1
Your T-shirt can be long-sleeved or a vest, patterned or plain. Go for whatever style you wish, but make sure it's stretchy. For the skirt part, choose a fabric that will match (think a black tee with a black skirt), or contrast (any one for yellow and purple?). The best thing about this project is that you decide *all* the elements.

STEP 2
Put the fabric you will use in the washing machine before you start to get rid of any excess dye and make it easier to work with. An iron wouldn't hurt, either.

STEP 3
Do you want your dress to have an empire line, or for the T-shirt and skirt to meet at your waist? You could even go for a drop waist, so these two parts meet around your hips. Think about what style usually suits you best.

STEP 4
The next decision? The length. Do you want the skirt to come to your knee, or higher?

STEP 5
We start by making the skirt. On a traditional dress pattern you'd get the measurements for a size 10, 12 etc. But not so here. I know that women are different shapes and sizes, so I reckon the best way to get a dress that is perfect for your body shape is to experiment with scrap fabric and work out a personalised pattern from scratch. (You can buy some thin fabric for £2 a metre.)

STEP 6
The basic shape of the skirt is like a triangle, with the top point lopped off, and the base line curved. To get the width of that top line, use a tape measure to measure around your body where the T-shirt and skirt will meet. Divide that number by two, then add a couple of centimetres (or more, if you have larger boobs – remember, this skirt section will have to be able to fit over them). Draw this on to the fabric.

STEP 7

Then, work out how long the skirt section needs to be (measure the distance between where you want the T-shirt section to end and where you want the hem of the skirt to finish). Use this to work out how tall your lopped-off triangle must be. How wide the triangle is at the bottom depends on your hips and thighs; if they're not much bigger than your waist, your skirt will be less flared, if they're larger, it will need to be.

STEP 8

Your template is ready. Hurrah! Add 2cm (³⁄₄in) seams all the way around and cut it out from your scrap fabric twice, on the bias. Pin these pieces together along the two long edges, 2cm in (see, your skirt is taking shape). Next, pin this trial skirt on to the T-shirt (don't cut anything from the tee yet) and, very carefully, try it on.

STEP 9

How does it feel? Where it is too tight and too baggy? Do the two pieces need to be wider at some points, so the skirt is more like a bell shape than a triangle? Make notes, and make yourself a new template. Try that one out. (Be warned: it might take more than one attempt to get your template right, but it's worth it; scrap fabric doesn't cost much, and it'll be cheaper than making a costly mistake with the real – and pricey – material.)

STEP 10

Happy? Great. Draw around the final template on to your real fabric (on the bias) using tailor's chalk. Cut two pieces of this (you have 2cm seams still, right?).

STEP 11

Sew around all the raw edges of both skirt pieces with a narrow zigzag stitch (or, by hand, an over sew stitch). This will stop them from fraying in the wash.

STEP 12

Pin the two pieces together, right sides facing, and sew 2cm from the edge with a backstitch. Use an iron to press the seams open.

STEP 13

Finally, hem the bottom of the skirt. Fold 2cm up, press with an iron and either hem it (page 195) or backstitch. (You might need to cut a few slits in the seam, à la the seams class on page 21, to get a really neat fold.)

STEP 14

At last! You're ready to cut the T-shirt to your required length. Add 2cm on for seams, and cut straight across. Zigzag stitch, or oversew, the raw edges.

STEP 15

The next part requires a sewing machine. Hand-wind shirring elastic on to your bobbin (the general consensus is that if you do it with your machine, it stretches too much). Put normal, strong all-purpose thread on top of the machine. Set the stitches short.

STEP 16

Turn the T-shirt inside out, but keep the skirt the right way around. Pull the T-shirt over the skirt, so the skirt is inside and their edges are lined up. Pin these together, ensuring the side seams line up as best as possible.

STEP 17

Sew these two pieces together, 2cm from the edges of the fabric (you have got shirring elastic in the bobbin, I assume?).

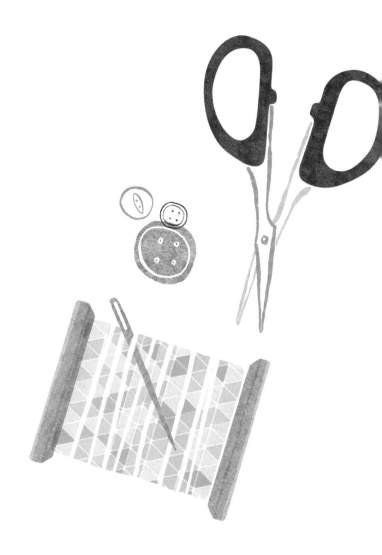

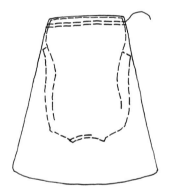

STEP 18

The base of your dress is all done. Good work. What else you add is up to you. A collar, perhaps (page 198)? Or some embellishments (page 116)? Have fun playing.

The extras

THE T-SHIRT YOU CAN TURN INTO ANYTHING

Find a baggy T-shirt in a colour or pattern you love and, with a few snips and stitches, it can become something entirely new that you might actually wear. Scenario one: chop the sleeves off, make it fitted, then cut a low round/v-neck (there's no need to worry about seams; T-shirt fabric doesn't fray too easily). Scenario two: do the same, but leave the neck high and add a new collar. Scenario three: cut from armpit to armpit so you're left with a tube. Make it fitted. Now sew a running stitch up the side, à la the ruffle on page 118, and gather up the sides to make a ruched strapless top. And finally, scenario four: cut large armholes and a large neck. Then, all the way along the bottom, every 1cm, snip up about 30cm, to give it a fringed edge. After doing all this you'll be left with a loads of fabric offcuts; you could use these to add matching embellishments.

FIVE WAYS WITH A LITTLE BLACK DRESS

Once you've mastered the basics of this chapter (and embellishing, on page 116, and encrusting, on page 68), you can pimp a plain dress a thousand different ways. Here are a handful of ideas.

✄ *Add a line of something up the back.* Be it a contrasting zip or ruffle, or a line of tiny bows, studs or safety pins, there's something elegant about detail on the back of a dress instead of the front.

✄ *Cover a single panel* entirely with sequins or giant discs. If might be the chest, a side section or the waistband. (Just make sure it's an area of your body that you like, as all eyes will be on this part.)

✄ *Play around with fringing.* (By fringing, of course, I mean something luxurious from a haberdashery, not the stuff from around your gran's lampshade.) Sew rows of it all around the bottom half of a dress, from the waistband downwards. Or, sew a few rows around the neck.

✄ *Make a statement strap.* Entirely cover one strap or sleeve with giant embellishments (fabric clusters made from silk or chiffon in the same colour as the dress can look magnificent). Or, add your own asymmetrical strap to a strapless dress. Take a length of ribbon or a hemmed strip of contrasting fabric, and stitch one end to the front (to the inside) and one to the opposite side of the back.

✄ *Learn how to drape.* Pin sections of the skirt up (with a humble safety pin) to create beautiful folds and creases and drapes. It might take a few attempts to get it right, but it'll be worth it.

MAKE STRAIGHT JEANS SKINNY

So long as jeans are fitted at the top, you can turn them into a new pair in an evening using a slightly altered version of the 'Make it fitted' technique on page 194. Turn them inside out and put them on. Pin up the inside leg, evenly, where you want the new seam to be (you shouldn't have to go past the knee). The key to avoiding the homemade look is to ensure that the outside seam is still running straight down the side of your leg. Check you've not pinned them so tight you can't get your foot out, then sew along the line of pins, very securely (use a size-14 sewing machine needle for medium-weight denim). Turn them the right way around, check they fit, then cut off the excess fabric 1cm from the seam.

'BE TRUE
TO YOURSELF!'

Craft your own business

It's never been easier to make money from making. Here are a few nuggets of advice from the people who have made a success of it …

INSIDER TRICKS FOR …

Crafting your collection

✂ *Craft your collection carefully.* Think about how you will stand out. What's your unique selling point? 'Sell a few things that relate to each other,' says **Georgina Blain** of Etsy, the world's largest handmade marketplace *(etsy.com)*. 'You don't want lots of random things otherwise people don't know what you're about.' Mix cheaper products with more expensive things, so that you have something for buyers with all budgets. When you've made your core products the best they can be, add new things to keep loyal customers interested, she advises.

✂ *Price it right.* Don't try to compete with the high street, she explains. 'People are willing to pay a bit more for handmade.' Factor in the cost of materials and your time, and there's your price tag. 'Don't be afraid of charging what you think is right. There will be people who will pay £5 for a scarf, and some who will pay £200.'

✂ *Don't lose your passion.* Set aside time to make stuff that isn't for sale, so you don't end up resenting your hobby. It's good business sense, too, Georgina says. 'Don't get bogged down churning out the same thing, else you won't be able to take your brand to the next level. Retain some of your creativity.'

Selling online

✂ *Tell your story.* 'Product description should have the core facts (size, colour, etc.) with a touch of the makers personality, says **Carrie Tucker**, of Not On The Highstreet *(notonthehighstreet.com)*. 'Describe how the item is made, highlight the emotional side to the process. Making the customer feel connected to the item helps make the sale.'

✂ *Use brilliant photos.* 'It's essential that the customer can get as much information as possible through a photo,' she explains. Shoot in situ and from different angles. Use a good digital camera and position things in natural light (or skill-swap with a local photographer).

✂ *Consider every last detail.* 'First impressions count,' she says. 'The packaging needs to reflect the care with which the product has been made.' Wrap things as beautifully as you can: nice tissue paper, a little ribbon and a handwritten note should help your customers remember you next time they want to shop online.

Making a craft fair work for you

✂ *Learn how to stand out.* You'll have a flat table and your imagination to work with, says **Victoria Woodcock**, head honcho at London's Bust Craftacular fair. 'It's easier to attract people when you sell big things like cushions, but not when it's little things like jewellery.' Arrive in good time and plan your set-up well: display products on platforms (boxes draped with fabric works well), use lighting to focus attention on smaller pieces, and create atmosphere however you can, she says.

✂ *Be approachable.* 'Part of the appeal of a craft fair is that you can chat to the person that made the thing that you're buying,' she says. 'Don't sit there in a strop, but equally don't stand over everyone saying "Please, please buy my things".'

✂ *Bring the essentials.* A wheelie case to transport your gear, plenty of spare change and business cards (people might not buy from you now, but might online later).

Getting into shops

✂ *Be brave.* 'When I started I naively picked up the phone to Paul Smith and asked if the buyers would like to see my stuff,' explains **Lisa Stickley**, a textile designer who took her business from her bedroom to big department stores (*lisastickley-levis.tumblr.com*). They bought 32 bags. Her advice is: if your products are good enough, retailers will want to stock them. Just don't take any orders you can't fulfil.

✂ *Learn the ropes.* 'In meetings with buyers you'll talk about what you'll make from it and what they'll make for it,' she says. Know the difference between cost price (what the retailer buys it from you for) and retail price (what they sell it for). Smaller local stores will probably just take the goods you produce, but larger stores and chains might have a hand in the design. 'It's a collaborative process,' she adds.

✂ *Get used to designing commercially.* If a retailer will only buy a bag from you for £20 and (factoring in your time and materials) it costs you £25 to make it, something has to give. Do you choose less pricey fabric or spend less time on sewing? 'A good designer has to be able to design within those constraints and be creative with solving those problems,' Lisa says.

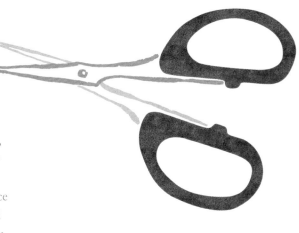

Become a craft tutor

✄ *Know your stuff.* 'While a lengthy CV might be impressive, a working knowledge of the subject at hand far more important,' says **Jennifer Pirtle**, founder of craft studio The Make Lounge (*themakelounge. com*). You needn't have a degree or any special qualifications, but you must know your stuff.

✄ *Have a passion for people.* 'Do you feel energized and self-assured when speaking in front of a group?' Jennifer asks. Because that's what she wants from her tutors. 'A good teacher feels comfortable while imparting information; students pick up on nervousness and can find it distracting.'

Get paid for blogging

✄ *Write well, and often.* 'The most important thing is that you have quality content', says **Lisa Lam** of U Handbag (*u-handbag.com*). Write interesting posts, and readers (and links back to your blog) will come. 'It's worth putting up three posts every week.'

✄ *Tell the world you take adverts.* 'I have a tab with all the key information on,' she says. However, how much you disclose publicly is up to you. 'Some bloggers have their rates public, others don't.' Expect interested parties to ask how many hits you get and what continent these are from (your blog stats and Google Analytics will tell you this).

✄ *Stay on top of the admin.* 'You need to be organised. Pay attention to when people need to stump up money, or when you have to take ads off.' Lisa doesn't have contracts with companies that advertise ('I think it puts the smaller sellers off'), just agreements for whether the ad is up for one, three or six months.

Open a craft shop/ studio/café

✄ *Start small.* You needn't buy premises straight away. 'Run workshops or sell things out of your home or sell from one of those pop-up shops where the rent is free for a couple of months,' suggests **Louise Hall**, founder of the Papered Parlour (*thepaperedparlour.co.uk*). 'Start it as a side venture to test how it goes.'

✄ *Have more than passion.* 'You take on everything, from processing bookings to sourcing future classes to the accounts, so some business sense is vital.' If you don't have that, get it. Louise owns the Papered Parlour with **Claire Heafford**, and has found the partnership a huge success. 'We have different and complementary skills that bring different things to the business.'

Appliqué

An age-old technique for decorating textiles with, well, smaller bits of textile. It certainly looks a lot better than it sounds.

The technique

MATERIALS

1 **A base**
You can appliqué on to any textile, from the front of a duvet to a purse.

2 **Fabric**
It's from this that you'll cut the shape to be appliquéd. Felt is brilliant, because it doesn't fray. Anything stretchy or too thick is difficult to work with.

3 **Multipurpose thread/embroidery thread**

4 **Fusible webbing**
Buy sheets with a paper backing, not thin strips, and always follow the instructions on the packet.

5 **Pins**

6 **Fabric scissors**

7 **Iron**

8 **See-through plastic sewing machine foot**
A normal sewing foot does the job, but if you use this, you can see what you're stitching more easily.

GETTING STARTED

Do you want to make a feature of the stitches, or hide them away? This will dictate which of the following methods you use. Whichever you go for, think carefully about where you place the appliqué. Do you want it slap bang in the middle of a cushion, or off-centre? Do you want shapes randomly dotted on the outside of a bag, or following the curve of the edge?

I DON'T WANT TO SEE THE STITCHES …

… and my appliqué fabric doesn't fray
Transfer your design on to the paper side of a piece of fusible webbing (draw it or use one of the techniques on page 22), but don't cut it out just yet. Place the appliqué fabric right-side down and lay the webbing on top: iron to stick it, as per the instructions on the packet (see page 20 for more details). Once cool, cut it out. Now, peel the paper backing off and lay it on your base, right-side up. Iron it on, again following the instructions, and you're done.

… and my fabric does fray
Transfer your appliqué design on to a piece of thin paper, and cut it out. Lay it on the back of your appliqué fabric, draw around it, add a ½cm

seam and cut that out. (Snip any curved seams or corners, as page 21.)

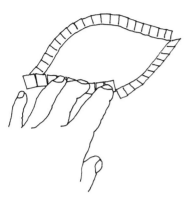

Fold the seams over the paper, and press in place with an iron. Remove the paper. Pin the appliqué on to the right side of your base fabric and, using tiny oversew stitches, sew it on.

I DEFINITELY WANT TO SEE THE STITCHES

Pin the pre-cut appliqué in place (or, to make stitching a hell of a lot easier, attach it using fusible webbing, as above), and …

✂ *Sew it on by hand* using a backstitch or running stitch, a couple of millimetres from the edge. Expect ragged edges over time if you're using fabric that frays.

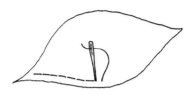

✂ *Set your sewing machine* to a long, narrow zigzag stitch, and sew around the edge. Secure the thread as normal or use the tying method for a neater finish (on page 18).

✂ *Try blanket stitch.* Using embroidery thread, poke your needle up through the appliqué, about $1/2$cm from the edge. Poke it back into the fabric 5mm to the left of where it came in, and bring the point of the needle up out again, as above right. This point should pass in front of the thread, as illustrated. Keep going like this and you'll soon see your blanket stitch take shape. Traditional blanket stitch

has evenly spaced stitches of the same length, but you could make a feature of using stitches of different lengths.

TO FINISH

Give your decorated fabric an iron (if it's delicate fabric, or you've got visible stitching, lay a tea towel on top first and iron through that).

COMMON PROBLEMS

My fusible webbing doesn't stick/ has covered my iron in goo. You've got the webbing the wrong way round. The shiny side should be touching the back of the fabric. Or, you've bought a non-paper-backed webbing.

Argh! My fabric has frayed. I'm afraid this is what happens when you use the wrong method of appliqué. Embrace the rough-around-the-edges look, or unpick and start again. This time, if you simply must use a fabric that frays (and can't/won't use the right method, above), invest in no-fray fabric spray.

The masterclass

JAN CONSTANTINE

ON STYLISH APPLIQUÉ

YOU CAN FIND JAN'S CLASSIC APPLIQUÉ HOMEWARES
IN THE FINEST DEPARTMENT STORES IN THE COUNTRY:
HARRODS, SELFRIDGES, LIBERTY AND FORTNUM &
MASON. *janconstantine.com*

BACK TO BASICS

'Try a very simple project first. Do something with your name, or your initial. A heart is possibly the most effective shape,' she says. 'You don't have to do the most intricate, detailed stuff. The simple designs can work.' It's worth putting a bit of extra effort into making sure your heart or lettering is the perfect shape before you cut it out.

THINK CAREFULLY ABOUT FABRIC

'You have to balance patterned fabric with plain,' she says. If your appliqué material is very patterned, go for a plainer base fabric, and vice-versa.

IT'S NOT ALL ABOUT COLOUR

'In the early days I started off working with a lot of white and cream because I couldn't afford other fabrics. So I used texture. I've done a velvet cushion in cream, and on it placed a cream wool appliqué. The shine from the velvet and the matte of the wool worked so well.'

INSIDER TRICKS

'I do appliqué with raw edges, so picking the right fabric is key – brushed cottons and winceyettes work beautifully, as they don't fray too much.'

POPPY TREFFRY, TEXTILE DESIGNER

poppytreffry.co.uk

'Having trouble tracing your appliqué shape on to slippery fabric? Place a piece of fine-grain sand paper underneath the fabric to hold it in place.'

MICHELLE DUXBURY, CRAFT WRITER FOR DOMESTIC SLUTTERY

domesticsluttery.com

'Look at the fabrics you have carefully. Cut out the patterns that appeal to you and use these as appliqués rather than creating your own. Collage, layer up, overlap, rotate and play with these fabrics until you've made a completely unique piece of work.'

CHLOE OWENS, TEXTILE DESIGNER

chloeowens.com

The project

SILHOUETTE APPLIQUÉ ART

So you're no Picasso. So what? A masterpiece needn't be painted to look magnificent, and appliqué is a simple way to stitch something great.

HOW HARD IS IT TO DO?

The sewing is the easy bit. It's the folding that can get tricky.

HOW LONG DOES IT TAKE?

Stick to something simple and you can be done in an hour. A stag should take a long afternoon.

MATERIALS

1. Paper
2. Pen
3. Fusible webbing/fabric stabiliser
4. Tailor's chalk
5. Fabric
6. Iron
7. Mounted canvas
8. Needle
9. Thread
10. Masking tape

STEP 1

Choose your silhouette. Anything that is recognisable from its outline will work, such as a palm tree or a bird. Trace a shape/object/picture that you find on the internet, or draw something freehand. (Find a template for my stag's head on page 220 – photocopy it and enlarge it to the size you want, though I reckon it looks best on a large 70cm by 70cm (28in by 28in) canvas.)

STEP 2

Draw around your silhouette on the paper side of fusible webbing or fabric stabiliser. Cut this out, then iron it to the back of a piece of lovely fabric. Mark a line all the way around the webbing shape, 1cm ($^1/_2$in) from the edge, using tailor's chalk. Cut out the fabric along this line.

STEP 3

What we're doing is a variation of the 'I-don't-want-to-see-the-stitches-and-my-fabric-does-fray' appliqué method on page 212. Rather than folding the 1cm seam over a piece of paper (which would be fiddly), we're folding it over webbing, which is fixed to the fabric so doesn't move at all. Refresh you're memory of the seams class on page 21, and snip triangles and slits on the curves and corners of the seam allowance where necessary.

STEP 4

Work your way around the edge of the silhouette, ironing the 1cm seam over as you go. This is most fiddly at the detailed sections (such as the antlers). Use pins or pieces of masking tape to hold the folded seam in place, if needed. This step will take the most time, but get it right and it makes the next step much easier. Once done, the silhouette will be the same shape and size as the template you drew in the first step.

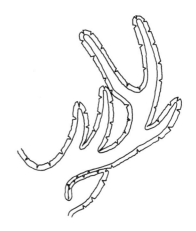

STEP 5

Position your appliqué on to the canvas, and hold it in place with masking tape (I find pins stretch the fabric). Oversew it on, all the way around, with about 1cm between each stitch. You will have to do battle with a couple of wooden planks at the back of the canvas, but with a bit of jiggery pokery, you'll get your needle in there.

The extras

STAY ICONIC, OR ADD A TOUCH OF HUMOUR

There's no denying it: appliqué can look incredibly naff if you get it wrong. My advice? When embellishing clothes or homewares, use any technique but blanket stitch (it's too folksy) and stick to iconic or amusing designs. Think postage stamps or giant red lips on cushions or tea cosies, and moustaches or polka dots on the front of a jumper or a make-up bag. Avoid anything too cute or twee, such as flowers, houses, beach scenes and butterflies.

ALL THE SMALL THINGS

It's the details that make a house a home, and appliqué is an easy way to create little decorations that can be hung from door handles or hooks (or at Christmas, from the tree). Make a simple paper template (a heart or a bird, for instance) and use it to cut two shapes from felt. Decorate these with appliqué (add a smaller heart in the centre, or the wing of the bird). Pin the two pieces together, right sides facing. Fold a short piece of ribbon in half, poke it between the layers of felt where you want the hanging loop to be and pin in place. (Remember, you're going to turn this inside out, so at this point the loop should be inside the shape, and the ends of the ribbon on the outside). Sew around the edge, leaving a 3cm (1$\frac{1}{4}$in) opening, and turn the right way around. Stuff with stuffing or lavender or similar, then stitch the hole closed with oversew stitches.

DOWN WITH THE KIDS

You can have the most fun with appliqué when using it to make stuff for young children (you can get away with bright colours and blanket stitch). Embellish a plain T-shirt with their name, the pocket of a dress with their favourite animal or a pair of gloves with a flower. Or, get your teeth stuck into a bigger project and appliqué a large design to a plain piece of cotton, to be framed and hung in their room (the alphabet, done in block letters, is always a classic).

Templates

The design I used to block-print my scarf on page 60.
Trace this, and use the technique on page 22 to transfer it on to your own block.

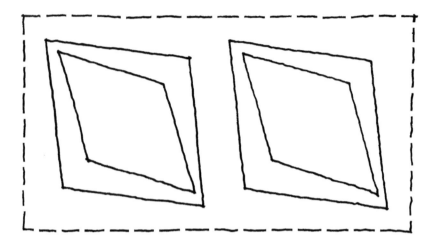

The alphabet cross-stitch chart for the bag project on page 83.
One black square equals one cross stitch (but remember for this large pattern, one cross stitch is made across four squares, not one).

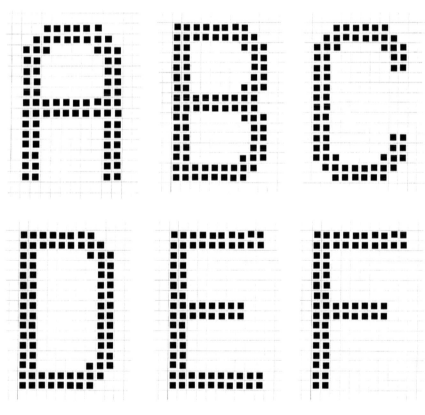

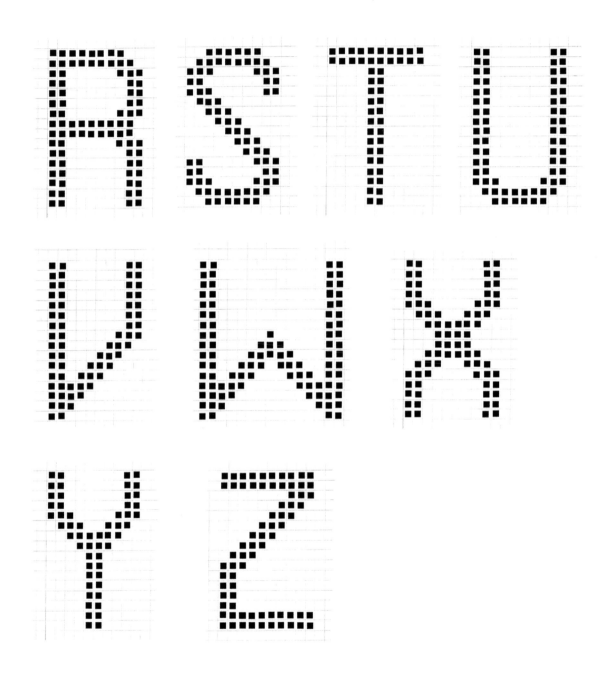

The stag template for my appliqué art project on page 213.
Use a photocopier to enlarge this. Or, take a photo, enlarge it on
your computer, then print it out in sections and sticky-tape together.

Material world

THE DIRECTORY

THE SHOPS

✂ Your local haberdasher should be your first stop for all things sewing; they'll have the basics (notions, trims and fabric) and the know-how to solve all kinds of craft dilemmas. Failing that, John Lewis haberdasheries have had a massive overhaul in recent years and are now almost restored to their former glory (I've always found their sewing-machine service impeccable) (*johnlewis.com*). Nationwide, larger Paperchase stores are brilliant for fancy paper and paints (*paperchase.co.uk*) and for crafting basics, there's always Hobbycraft.

✂ A trip to London isn't complete without a look around Liberty's famed haberdashery on Regent Street, where you'll find the world's biggest supply of Liberty print fabrics and much more. Just around the corner is Berwick Street, home to a host of fabric shops, and MacCulloch and Wallis (*macculloch-wallis. co.uk*) which has three floors of haberdashery. The five Cass Art shops will sort out all your cross stitching and printing needs, the two VV Rouleux stores

(*vvrouleaux.com*) have the most stylish selection of ribbons and trims, and Covent Garden's Beadworks (*beadworks.co.uk*) sells all the tools and materials you need to make your own jewellery.

✂ Across the country there are plenty of great local craft stores, but some stand out for their superb collection of products, beautiful décor and general dedication to craft wonderfulness. Should you pass anywhere near them I suggest you take a detour. Hurrah for Millie Moon in Froome, Somerset (*milliemoonshop.co.uk*); Lexi Loves in Cirencester, Gloucestershire (*lexilovesshop. com*) and The Eternal Maker in Chichester, West Sussex (*eternalmaker.com*). Kudos to Fred Aldous, the family-run craft superstore in Manchester (*fredaldous.co.uk*), and The Bead Shops in Scotland, too (*beadshopscotland.co.uk*).

ONLINE

✂ Buy and sell handmade products at *Etsy.com, Folksy.com, SeekandAdore.com, CraftNation. com, PapaStour.com, Misi.co.uk* or *WowThankYou.co.uk*

✂ Get your mitts on brilliant fabrics and trims at *Backstitch co.uk, FancyMoon.co.uk, JosyRose.com, Seamstar.co.uk, AmyButlerDesign.com, MyFabricHouse.co.uk, FabricRehab.co.uk* and *MisForMake.co.uk. PixieRose.co.uk* and *LupinHandmade.com* are especially good for felt. Or, have personalised material printed at UK-based *TheFabricPress.com* or US-based *SpoonFlower.com* For leather, I like eBay or *PittardsLeather.co.uk*.

✂ For buttons, try *ButtonCompany. co.uk, ButtonMad.com, handmadebybutton.com* and *SewBox.co.uk*. Beads (and plenty of jewellery-making supplies) can be found at *BeadMerchant. co.uk, TheBeadStalk.co.uk, EmpireBeads.co.uk, TheBeadStore. co.uk, LondonBeadCo.co.uk* and *BeadsUnlimited.co.uk*.

✂ There are an lot of awful paper supplies on the web, but I like *CreativePaperWales.co.uk* (for paper made from Welsh sheep poo), *EcoPaper.com* (for recycled sheets) and *JJQuilling.co.uk* (for quilling supplies).

And finally, buy beautifully packaged sewing supplies at *MerchantAndMills.com* and Sheffield-made scissors at *ErnestWright.co.uk*.

THE WORKSHOPS

✂ London has a fine array of craft studios: The Make Lounge in Islington *(themakelounge.com)*, Homemade London just off Oxford Street *(homemadelondon. com)*, Fabrications in Hackney *(fabrications1.co.uk)* and in Clapham, The Papered Parlour *(thepaperedparlour.co.uk)* and Sew Over It *(sewoverit.co.uk)*. For millinery courses (and supplies), there's Atelier Millinery *(atelier-millinery.com)*, for jewellery-making, try Hatton Garden's London Jewellery School *(londonjewelleryschool.co.uk)*, and bookbinding store Shepherds Falkiners *(store.falkiners.com)* does paper cutting, paper making, leather work and more. Short courses at the London College of Fashion are pricey, but come highly recommended *(fashion. arts.ac.uk)*.

✂ Outside the capital, Glasgow is spoiled for choice with Make it Glasgow *(makeitglasgow. co.uk)* and The Life Craft *(thelifecraft.co.uk)*. Birmingham has Creative Open Workshops *(creativeopenworkshops.com)* and in Manchester Ministry of Craft courses are held at Fred Aldous craft store *(ministryofcraft. co.uk)*. The Makery in Bath *(themakeryonline.co.uk)* is a fabulous space, as is Just Sew in Brighton *(justsewbrighton.co.uk)*.

THE REST

✂ Part-bar, part-gallery, part-shop, part-studio, London's Drink Shop Do *(drinkshopdo.com)* is a must-see destination for any crafter. Or if you're heading over to France, grab a coffee and rent a sewing machine at the original craft café in Paris, Sweat Shop *(sweatshopparis.com)*

✂ The Knitting and Stitching Show, held in London, Dublin and Harrogate *(twistedthread. com)* is the big daddy of craft shows, with stalls, galleries, workshops and a hell of a lot more. But if it's contemporary craftsmanship you're after, pay a visit to the Crafts Council's two annual London fairs, Origin *(originuk.org)* and COLLECT *(craftscouncil.org.uk/collect)*, or to the annual Great Northern Craft Fair *(greatnorthernevents.co.uk)*.

✂ The UK has some cracking centres for craft, too, which work tirelessly to promote makers and their work, and offer advice, gallery, studio and selling space. Drop in to London's Craft Central *(craftcentral.org.uk)* or Manchester's Craft and Design Centre *(craftanddesign.com)*, both non-for-profit organisations where you can sample a taster of that region's craft. Or keep an eye on Craftspace *(craftspace.co.uk)*, a roving not-for-profit based in Birmingham.

Acknowledgements

I raise a glass to each of these lovely people, without whom you would not be reading this book …

The *Guardian*'s Kate Carter and Rachel Dixon, who published my very first adventures in craft; Kate Shaw, my agent, who believed that I had a book in me; and Hannah Knowles, my editor, who took a chance on that book. Thank you for all for your support, and for letting me do craft the way I wanted to do it.

The many incredible contributors whose wisdom can be found throughout this book: never in my wildest dreams did I think so many people of your calibre would agree to be part of my little project. If any of you ever need anything, you've got my number. Massive props too to every maker, designer and craft blogger who has inspired me over the last five years. Had we had the space, I would have crammed so many more of you in this book.

Photographer Luke J. Albert and stylist Samara Tompsett, who transformed the stuff I made into a set of stunning photographs; Nina Ziegler, designer extraordinaire; Toby Clarke, for his excellent finishing skills; and illustrator Kate Wilson, whose work I have admired from afar for a very long time. Craft, in my opinion, has never looked so stylish,

and I take none of the credit for that. My amazing supporting cast. Dee, Fiona, Hannah, Heather, Jessica, Kate, Mel, Sam, the best BFFs anyone could ask for. The *Psychologies* team, who put up with my many freak-outs over the last 12 months – you are absolute legends. Josephine Lewis (aka Nana) and Sarah Griffiths (aka my late Gran), who taught me everything I know about making, and are better crafters than I could ever wish to be. And, of course, my mum and dad, Elaine and Phil Lewis (yes, Phil Lewis, *Material World*'s chief illustrator, is my dad). When I grow up I hope I am as supportive, inspiring, talented and generally as all-round awesome as you are. Thank you for everything.

Finally, to J, who has spent the last eighteen months quietly making my life as easy as possible so I could put all my energy into this project. Without him, there would be no *Material World*, and so this book is dedicated to him. Jonathon Cox, I owe you big time.

Many thanks to the following photographers for the kind reproduction of their images…

Page 32: Rémi Duval
Page 70: Eddie Monsoon
Page 82: Hotspot Media
Page 109: ID Sites
Page 121: Ruth Crafer
Page 133: Martin Evening
Page 170: Nick Knight
Page 171: Andreas von Einsiedel
Page 201: Stephanie Sian Smith
Page 214: Ray Main